THE USE OF EXPLOSIVE IDEAS
IN EDUCATION

OTHER BOOKS IN THE CLASSICS
IN PROGRESSIVE EDUCATION SERIES

Being with Children:
A High-Spirited Personal Account of Teaching Writing, Theater,
and Videotape
PHILLIP LOPATE

Diary of a Harlem Schoolteacher
JIM HASKINS

Fuller's Earth
A Day with Buckminster Fuller and the Kids
RICHARD J. BRENNEMAN

How Kindergarten Came to America:
Friedrich Froebel's Radical Vision of Early
Childhood Education
BERTHA VON MARENHOLTZ-BÜLOW

The New Education:
Progressive Education One Hundred Years Ago Today
SCOTT NEARING

The Public School and the Private Vision:
A Search for America in Education and Literature
MAXINE GREENE

Schoolmaster of the Great City:
A Progressive Educator's Pioneering Vision for
Urban Schools
ANGELO PATRI

THE USE OF
EXPLOSIVE IDEAS
IN EDUCATION

Culture, Class, and Evolution

THEODORE BRAMELD

THE NEW PRESS

NEW YORK
LONDON

Requests for permission to reproduce selections from this book
should be mailed to: Permissions Department, The New Press,
38 Greene Street, New York, NY 10013.

Originally published in the United States by the University of Pittsburgh Press, 1965
Published in the United States by The New Press, New York, 2008
Distributed by W. W. Norton & Company, Inc., New York

ISBN 978-1-59558-421-2 (pb)
CIP data available

The New Press was established in 1990 as a not-for-profit alternative to the large,
commercial publishing houses currently dominating the book publishing industry.
The New Press operates in the public interest rather than for private gain, and is
committed to publishing, in innovative ways, works of educational, cultural, and
community value that are often deemed insufficiently profitable.

www.thenewpress.com

Composition by NK Graphics,
a Black Dot Group Company
This book was set in New Caledonia

Printed in Canada

2   4   6   8   10   9   7   5   3   1

To the memory of T.V. Smith

Contents

SERIES FOREWORD
Classics in
Progressive Education

My first classroom was empty. Not a book, piece of paper, pencil, or stick of chalk was in sight. The principal welcomed me to the school and informed me he had high expectations for each and every student. Crazy. I figured I had to dig into my meager savings and buy pencils, some remaindered typing paper, and discount crayons. Books were out of the question.

It was rough going for my first week of teaching, but during my second, two older female teachers showed up in my classroom after school. It turns out they were watching me and decided I might be a lifer—a lifelong progressive education teacher. They brought me boxes of books, material about the United Federation of Teachers, and most of all, some classics of progressive education. Over coffee after school one day, they informed me that both of them would retire in a year but wanted to keep the tradition of democratic, student-centered education alive. These teachers hoped to keep arts in the schools and they hoped that young teachers like me (I was 23 at the time) would keep the tradition going. But, they emphasized, in order to keep a tradition alive, you had to know its history and read its literature. That's why, in addition to all the specific educational material these teachers brought me, they insisted I read Dewey, Froebel, Freinet, Homer Lane, Makarenko, and many other democratic educators whose work has had major influences on educators throughout the world. Their teaching was concrete and their vision for education was large.

I didn't have a chance to thank these two teachers because

they retired in the middle of my first year of teaching without leaving their names or addresses. But I have honored their commitment to children and to progressive education. This series is meant to show them my appreciation for their unsolicited gifts to me.

This series will reissue important but often hard-to-find works of progressive education which are still very useful to people teaching today. It is essential to connect to tradition, to know that you are not alone trying to fight against authoritarian or corporate education. The goal is to energize teachers through a connection to educators who have struggled for democratic and creative education against the demands of governments, the rigidity of some churches, and the complex lives many students are forced to bear. The books reprinted are for teachers of hope who understand the complexities of struggling for their students and who might need a dose of history, a bit of humor, and lots of new ideas.

—Herbert Kohl
February 2007

Foreword

Theodore Brameld (1904–1987) was one of the leading progressive educational philosophers of the twentieth century. He was born in Neillsville, Wisconsin, and graduated from Ripon College in 1926. He then studied educational philosophy at Teachers College, Columbia, and at the University of Chicago. At Chicago, where he was a doctoral student, he was introduced to pragmatism and John Dewey's thinking. Over the years he wrote articles and books on subjects as diverse as teachers' unions, organized labor, and workers' education. In 1945 he wrote *Minority Problems in the Public School,* a prescient book on the coming problems of segregation and inequalities that characterize public education in the United States.

Brameld was committed to intercultural and multicultural education. At the center of his philosophy was a sense of the power of education to achieve personal and cultural transformation. Schools, according to Brameld, could be the instruments of social transformation and the creation of an equitable and democratic world. He called this somewhat utopian orientation "reconstructionism." His philosophy echoes many of the ideas practiced at the Highlander Research and Education Center, founded by Myles Horton, who also attended the University of Chicago when Brameld was a student there. At the heart of Highlander's practice was the idea that people who suffered social and economic problems could solve those problems themselves when engaged in communal dialogue and action. Brameld's philosophy was not academic. He believed that philosophy existed to guide and to be engaged in social action. Toward the end of his life, Brameld founded the Hardscrabble Center, which was specifically modeled on the Highlander Center.

A central part of the program of resonstructionism was to create a worldwide, compassionate community without national borders, in line with the ideas of the World Federalist Movement. In the 1950s Brameld was worried about nuclear warfare, the arms race between the United States and the Soviet Union, racism, poverty, and anti-science bias. These issues shaped his writing and thinking. He considered reconstructionism an urgent educational need. For him it was a question of how young people could be brought into the process of thinking about what he believed was a dangerous situation for humanity. The goal of reconstructionism was to enable students to find moral and intelligent answers to problems confronting society.

During the 1930s Brameld, along with Harold Rugg, Merle Curti, George Counts, and others, was a member of a group of progressive educators who believed that the role of education was to transform society in ways that embodied social and economic justice. They were all influenced by John Dewey's early work and were instrumental in the development of the Progressive Education Association (PGA).

Formed in reaction to the authoritarian and rigid education that characterized much of schooling in the United States in the late 1900s, the PGA was founded in 1919 and lasted until 1955. Its central goal was the development of student-centered educational environments based on the principles of democracy and choice. All of the members agreed on the general goal despite their disagreements about strategies.

Within the PGA, two main factions predominated. One was the child development group, which was concerned with the way young children learn. Many of the leading people in this group, most of whom were women, were influenced by the kindergarten movement that dated back to Elizabeth Peabody, Friedrich Froebel, and the introduction of kindergartens in the United States.

The other group—the political wing—came to be known as the Social Frontier group, after a political and educational journal they published. Ted Brameld was a member of this group. Many of its members were involved in research and the evaluation of educational programs for middle and high school students. Alice Kelliher, a central member of the child development wing (who went on to teach at NYU and whom I visited in 1981 at her home in Vermont) confirmed the far left character of the political wing of the PGA, referring to Brameld, Rugg, and most of all Counts as "the socialist boys."

Counts's book *Dare the School Build a New Social Order?* (1932) forcefully advocated ideas developed by this group. In it Counts claimed that education is culture-based. Rather than children being born "free," as Rousseau would have it, their development is dictated by the social conditions into which they are born. According to Counts, "the most crucial of all circumstances conditioning human life is birth into a particular culture."* He also claimed that since education is historically and culturally based, it develops through the value systems that define that culture. According to him, "the real question is not whether imposition will take place, but rather from what source it will come."† He concluded that teaching is a political activity and that teachers "need to respond to the abiding interests of the people" rather than cater to middle and upper class students.‡ He and Brameld held social and economic justice to be central to the very enterprise of public education.

Another member of the socialist wing of the PGA, Harold Rugg, created a social studies curriculum entitled "Man and His Changing Society." When I was in high school in the early 1950s, we were required to take a class called "Problems of American Democracy," which came straight out of Rugg's work. The curricu-

---

*G.S. Counts, *Dare the School Build a New Social Order?* (New York: John Day, 1932), 11.

†Ibid.

‡Ibid.

lum was designed to assist students in thinking about social problems and speculating on ways of solving them. At one time the entire curriculum and the textbooks it produced were used by nearly a million students throughout the country. Now it is just about impossible to find a complete set of the books. (After twenty years of searching, I have only about 15 percent of the set.) Based on the books I did find, I believe they should be put back into the schools.

Rugg's books tried to analyze what he called the developing democracy in the United States. It dared question the idea that democracy in the United States worked well for everybody and raised the issues of class, gender, and race. Rugg believed that problems of American democracy must be studied in the schools and that the visions of a perfect and fixed democracy projected in most U.S. history textbooks was damaging to the spirit of social activism he hoped the school would create.

In 1940 the National Association of Manufacturers (NAM) announced that it would investigate school textbooks that were supporting communism and undermining the American way of life. The NAM joined the American Legion and a group of conservative organizations called the American Coalition. Together they claimed that the specter of collectivism was sneaking into the schools and that it was their role as "sentinels" to protect capitalist America. The target these groups selected for their most violent attacks were the Rugg textbooks. The American Legion banded together with business organizations to eliminate them. Despite a study by leading historians from Harvard and Dartmouth affirming that the texts did *not* distort the primary documents of United States history in any way, the books were eliminated in all but a few progressive private schools.

Brameld brought many of the ideas of the Social Frontier group as well as his vision of a worldwide democracy together in his book *The Use of Explosive Ideas in Education,* first published in 1965 by the University of Pittsburgh Press and long out of print. Brameld was an educational philosopher of a peculiar sort. He felt that philosophy should not be abstract and theoretical, but a guide to social and educational action for change. As he said about *Explosive Ideas*, "This book is primarily concerned with philosophy as living." Brameld hoped the book would demonstrate philosophy as a bridge between theory and practice. He structured it to explore three themes: culture, class, and evolution. In each chapter, he examines the themes in three ways. For example, in the chapter on class, he has three sections titled "What is culture?," "Cultural Philosophic Perspectives," and "The School as Agent of Culture."

All of the ideas explored in the book are looked at from these three vantage points: definition, critical thinking about the idea, and the way in which the ideas explored in the text can be transformed into school practice. I think that teacher education could use this schema so that prospective teachers would develop understanding, critical thinking, and a sense of how to translate analysis into practice.

One of the other aspects of Brameld's thinking embodied in this book is what he calls bridge building. Brameld wanted to create dialogue—to bring together opposing views without having explosive ideas dominated by irrational passion and irreconcilable conflict.

Brameld's desire to build bridges did not keep him from holding firm to his commitment to education for social change. During the one time I met him, when he was quite old, it was clear that he was both a romantic and a progressive. He believed that dialogue and critique could lead to a common feeling for social justice. I think this book can help us take a few steps toward that dream. At the very least, it will inspire many people to take up the struggle for an intelligent understanding of explosive ideas and incorporate them into the school curriculum.

—Herbert Kohl
September 2008

PREFACE

The internecine warfare that has been raging for years between academicians and educationists is both wasteful and absurd. The profession of education is a noble one. The service that teachers perform in helping young people to grow into mature responsible adults is worthy of highest commendation. Yet, the disdain in which they are frequently regarded by members of other professions, and even by those members of their own profession who happen to teach in colleges of liberal arts, is a tragic commentary upon the confusions of value that prevail in so much of our culture. On the one hand, virtually everyone approves of and lauds education, including the public schools. On the other hand, it is only too often true that teachers and others engaged in educational work are treated as professional inferiors and the schools that prepare them to engage in that work are held in contempt.

As one who came into professional education by way of graduate study and teaching in colleges of liberal arts, I can, I think, understand something of the motivations and attitudes prevailing in both camps. Certainly it is true that colleges of education are woefully unsatisfactory in their present typical policies and programs. Certainly it is equally true that liberal-arts faculties are filled with individuals who cherish their niches in the academic pecking order far more than their professional performances deserve. It does little good, however, merely to plead for more cooperation or greater tolerance and understanding on the part of both antagonists. What is necessary is forthright demonstrations on the part of both that each is necessary to the other if either is to be thoroughly effective. Educationists (and this term, in my vocabulary, is *not* invidious) need to draw much more deeply and solidly from the resources of the liberal arts in revamping their own programs. Academicians need to learn that, if they are ever to be really competent teachers, they will have to benefit by strong theoretical and practical preparation in this kind of competence. The award of the Doctor of Philosophy degree no more necessarily qualifies a person to become a thoroughly expert teacher than would the award of a Doctor of Medicine degree qualify a person for his profession if he had never experienced clinical practice.

This book is an attempt to build a more vital rapprochement between educationists and academicians by drawing them together within a single large framework. In the degree that it succeeds in communicating its aims, it demonstrates that novel opportunities for fruitful interrelationships are now becoming available. Ultimately, this is a book in philosophic theory. Unlike most works in philosophy, however, it is almost equally a book in the liberal arts as well as a book in the practice of education. Its primary purpose is to bring the resources of these three fields together because all of them are imperative to the task of professional education in our day.

I could not have written it without a great deal of help. Much of this help will be apparent in the abundant intellectual resources that every chapter draws upon. In addition, I am indebted to colleagues in the Department of Educational Foundations at Boston University who contributed greatly to the development of the overall design, who helped to test it out, and who criticized early manuscript drafts. I wish especially to thank Professors Gene Phillips, Albert Kahn, Richard Rapacz, and James Chambliss (now at Rutgers University). Many students with whom the design was shared have also offered excellent suggestions, but one in particular has directly helped in preparing the bibliography and in other ways: Mr. Nobuo Shimahara, Fellow in the Human Relations Center at Boston University. My wife, Ona Brameld, has also assisted me faithfully as she has in the preparation of other books. Finally, I am grateful to Professor Robert Mason and other friends at the University of Pittsburgh who invited me to publish this book under their auspices.

May I respectfully underscore to the reader one word of guidance that I make in the course of the chapters? This is that he conscientiously supplement this book with the kind of resources for additional reading that are frequently provided. As anyone will quickly perceive who is at all informed in the fields where we shall concentrate, the attempt to encompass so much in so little space inevitably results in omissions, distortions, and oversimplifications. The impact of the concepts to be given chief attention is so prodigious that many books could be written about each—indeed, have already been written. Because, however, no reader is likely to follow all of the leads provided, I especially urge that where limited choices are essential these be made among the most original and basic authorities that I have cited. There is no substitute for them.

With scarcely an exception, I have made a point of including at least one writing from virtually every person named anywhere in the text. The reader can thus more easily trace the reasons for their influence.

For anyone who may find some of the terms technical and unfamiliar, I have also tried to define all of the important ones the first time they are used.

If the attempt here to break down obsolete barriers proves promising, other writers in educational theory are urged to tackle different crucial ideas through similary integrative frameworks. The task has only begun.

—Theodore Brameld

THE USE OF EXPLOSIVE IDEAS
IN EDUCATION

I

EDUCATION,

PHILOSOPHY, AND

THE POWER OF IDEAS

1

THE BRIDGES OF THEORY
AND PRACTICE

Philosophy as Lore or Living

Professor T. V. Smith, one of the great American teachers of philosophy, once delivered a memorable lecture for undergraduates at the University of Chicago. Its title was "Philosophy as Lore or Living." By lore he meant, of course, the way of the professional student of thought who studies ideas "for their own sake." Such a philosopher is not unlike artists who paint pictures "for their own sake" or mathematicians who pursue mathematical puzzles with no regard whatever for their possible practical usefulness. The philosopher of lore, then, is likely to be a person fascinated by the sheer complexity of, let us say, logical propositions or metaphysical abstractions. The history of philosophy is studied, not for any particular impact it might have made upon man's struggles, but as a brilliant history of the exercise of intellect.

The study of philosophy as lore is common in the universities of America, Europe, and Asia. Students often take courses from professors of philosophy who regard their subject matter to be primarily one of intricate patterns of thought that may have a fascination in and for themselves. It would be difficult to count the proportion of professional philosophers concerned primarily with their subject as lore. But it is probable that the percentage is considerably higher than the alternative group, which looks upon philosophy chiefly as living.

What might be meant by this latter phrase? Philosophy as living, as Professor Smith discussed it, is concerned with man's way—or more exactly, ways—of life. Therefore, it is inextricably bound up with the myriad of daily problems that confront ordinary people and, above all, with the beliefs by means of which they act upon such problems.

Many philosophers of this kind may be quite as professional as their colleagues of lore. Their teaching and writing are sometimes profound and even highly technical. But they differ in the sense that they are constantly confronted with firing-line issues of political, religious, economic, moral, and other dimensions of living experience. For them, the significance of any belief is tested by its relevance to such experience.

Smith did not for a moment deny that philosophers of lore have important contributions to make to civilization. So, too, do the so-called "pure" mathematicians or "pure" artists. Also, he surely would insist that the separation between lore and living is by no means as sharp as any simple discussion of the problem might tempt one to suppose. Many philosophers of lore have at least a secondary interest in problems of living and, certainly, most significant philosophers of living have a deep respect for philosophy as lore. Indeed, each group may draw upon the resources of the other in order to deal successfully with their own foci of interest.

Nor should it be forgotten that some of the greatest philosophers in history have managed to combine the two functions into a remarkable amalgam. In certain ways the great triumvirate of Greek philosophy—Socrates, Plato, and Aristotle—were men of practical living as well as profound thinkers in their own right. One thinks of the Roman emperor Marcus Aurelius, who was also a first-rate philosopher and one of the foremost contributors to the still influential theory of Stoicism. One thinks, too, of such modern philosophers as John Locke and Jean Jacques Rousseau, or, in the United States, of men like Thomas Jefferson and Justice Oliver Wendell Holmes.

A word should also be said concerning creative geniuses who have expressed their beliefs through media other than formal philosophic symbols. We are thinking here of such classical musicians as Beethoven and Chopin, of such contemporary painters as Blum and Picasso, and of such American poets as Walt Whitman and Robert Frost. However varied otherwise, their interpretations of man and the world are immersed in the stream of human struggle—of tragedy and comedy. They feel life deeply. They seek, above all, to come to grips with it through their own distinctive forms of expression.

The philosopher of lore is enriched by the philosopher of living, and the converse is equally true. Nevertheless, like such philosophers and artists as have just been mentioned, this book is concerned primarily with philosophy as living.

The Conflict Between Theory and Practice in Education

Let us attempt to state the problem of lore and living in another way. Assuming that philosophy is the most comprehensive of all forms of theory, how does one relate theory to practice so that theory makes a real difference *to* practice and is in turn improved *by* practice?

In education, as much as in any field of human experience, this question is persistent and troublesome. Most teachers are eager to perform effectively in their everyday work. Yet, in their very eagerness, in their need for down-to-earth hour-by-hour techniques of teaching and learning, do they always understand why they are doing what they do? Do they clearly grasp the purposes for which they act *as* they act? Do they perceive the network of relations of the particular facts or skills that they teach to the more general obligations of education? Above all, do they recognize that education is never just an activity in and for itself but is, rather, an invention of the human species designed to improve its lot in the wider environment of society, nature, and even the universe?

Questions such as these, granting their elusiveness and immensity, underscore the reasons why theory is anything but the futile luxury that so-called "commonsense" educators often claim it is. These educators, impatient as they are with anything that seems impractical or inapplicable to specific and immediate results, are in wider perspective themselves the most impractical of men. Because of their impatience, they are responsible in no small degree for the prodigious waste of educational resources, for confusing and conflicting activities, for meaningless requirements and sterile learnings. Over and over, they substitute short-term results for long-range achievements. And if they happen to be professors who emphasize research, too often are they likely to concentrate upon some minute segment of educational behavior, to engage in elaborate rituals of measuring that behavior and, finally, to produce nothing that makes any appreciable difference to educational advancement unless it be their precious list of publications.

It is only fair to point out, however, that educational theory suffers from severe limitations of its own. The accusation of educational practitioners that innumerable theorists get caught in their web of speculative lore is only too deserved. Or, to change the metaphor, the "ivory tower" can surely become quite as futile a retreat from reality as "common sense" can become an excuse for triviality and narrowness. That some philosophers are intellectually or emotionally incapable of the hard-headed often-bruising experience of direct involvement in, for example, administrative responsibilities is just as true as the fact that some practitioners are equally incapable of the patient arduous work of thinking through and then clearly stating a significant idea.

The point we are making is simple but crucial. The conflict between theory and practice is a false conflict. Practice in education needs theory in education, and theory equally needs practice. There is futile sterile practice. There is futile sterile theory. But neither need be so, and both can become fruitful and vital in partnership.

The Multidisciplinary Approach

Assuming, at least for purposes of argument, that the statements thus far are reasonable enough, new questions immediately loom. How is it possible to bring philosophic theories into dynamic connection with theories of, let us say, science or art? How, in turn, are these theories to be related to the practice of particular sciences or particular arts? And, finally, how can philosophy, the sciences, and arts come to bear directly upon the myriad activities of classrooms, playgrounds, administrative offices, and the communities that support all of these activities?

Even if education had not been growing at such a prodigious pace in America and other countries, it is unlikely that anyone could claim to have a final answer to a single one of these questions. We find little agreement, for example, as to which among several influential philosophies of education is the most authoritative. The theories, moreover, that underlie education in science or in art are frequently fuzzy, but even when they are fairly clear they too are probably in disagreement oftener than not. One consequence, of course, is that curricula, methods of learning, and patterns of administrative control frequently suffer from confusions and inconsistencies. Education today is often called a hodgepodge.

One possible way toward less confusion and more consistency is to recognize with increasing numbers of scholars that the time has come to begin earnestly to reverse a trend. This is the trend toward increasing specialization.

All of us are aware of how the medical profession, to take one instance, has proliferated into a thousand-and-one highly skilled competencies; all of us recognize, too, that medicine has made enormous advances as it has moved away from the traditional family doctor to the heart diagnostician or brain surgeon, and then to a hundred or more subdivisions of each such specialization. Thus, to speak of the need to "reverse a trend" is not to say that specialization should be opposed. Perhaps the term "reverse" is not quite accurate; "counterbalance" might be more so. For what we are urging, along with specialization in philosophy, science, art, and education is *inter*specialization—in short, a way by which each particular field can be brought into relationship with other fields. Let us call this the *multidisciplinary* approach.

Certainly, no one denies the desirability of manifold disciplines. But need they be so completely separate from or even so ignorant of one another as now often seems to be the case?

In common with the ancient view of philosophy as the attempt to view the world in a comprehensive vision, the time is ripe to search again for opportunities to unify the disparate parts of knowledge and experience. Indeed, the time is imperative.

We say "imperative," and our principal reason is a highly practical one. The specializations of modern knowledge—atomic physics most notably, of course—have produced a situation of unprecedented danger to human survival. No informed student need be reminded what this danger consists of. Nor should he have to be persuaded that the only hope for the world of avoiding the most dreadful of catastrophes is through a community of nations strongly organized enough to control any threat to the peace and security of mankind.

As the Preamble to the Constitution of UNESCO so eloquently reminds us, wars begin in the minds of men. But so, too, does peace begin in the minds of men. Peace is possible only when the people of nations and cultures understand not only their own natures but also the attitudes, habits, and institutions of people very different from themselves.

Such understandings start at home, however, and herein lies a foremost reason for the needed multidisciplinary counterbalance to the splintering of knowledge. For unless students of a great profession such as education can understand and appreciate the powerful ideas of philosophy, science, or art that are typical of their own culture, how can they be expected to understand and appreciate the ideas of people belonging to radically diverse cultures? Nor is it a matter of ideas merely. True enough, as already suggested, the ideas of theory are indispensable to practice. But equally true is the fact that ideas emerge from and are tested by the social, political, religious, and other practices of cultures everywhere.

Toward a Multidisciplinary Model

Still, it is not enough to contend that education has a major responsibility to search for ways of integrating knowledge. There is, of course, nothing new about this contention; proponents of "general education" have been urging it in different manners for a long time. What is needed in addition are graphic "models" of integration—the term "model" being used somewhat as an astronomer does when he builds an artificial solar system or as an architect does when he draws a blueprint for a new factory. In short, we need to experiment with systematized designs by which to draw together some of the specializations of knowledge and to relate them both to one another and to education.

The model we choose to construct consists of three interconnected bridges. On the left is the bridge of the arts and sciences: the great body of theory, knowledge, and creative achievement encompassed by these fields. On the right is the bridge of educational practice: the daily work of the student, teacher, and administrator—in short, the program of the typical college and school. In the middle is the bridge of philosophy: it connects the disciplines of the sciences and arts on the left side of the model with educational practice on the right side.

But what do all three connecting bridges connect with in turn? Let us answer by next imagining the two shores of a wide river. On both shores the actual lives of people go on—that is, their struggles to survive, to reproduce, to improve themselves; their loves and hates, their passions and superstitions, their customs and rituals. To adapt a term from the great American philosopher John Dewey, to whom we shall later refer, these are the shores of "immediate experience"—the direct, intense, often agonizing, sometimes ecstatic life that human beings everywhere on earth have always suffered and enjoyed.

People, however, are also notoriously restless. They are forever questing, forever daring to venture into the unknown. The records of archaeology—recall the *Kon-Tiki* expedition—are astonishing proof of the curiosity of men to cross, not merely rivers, but vast oceans and continents in search of something different, something wiser, something more hopeful. Occasionally they succeed; often they do not. But whatever their achievements we may be sure that such adventurers are never the same afterward. They have learned, and what they have learned they bring back home, adding to and modifying the immediate experiences that they had shared before.

Thus we observe a great deal of two-way traffic across these imaginary spans. Not only do many adventurers return enriched, or at least chastened, but groups from the farther side often follow them back in order to make new homes and grow new families. Thereby the races of the world have intermingled throughout aeons of time—so much so that prescientific notions of racial "purity" are now quite meaningless.

So, too, are the common notions regarding the "purity" of knowledge in philosophy, science, art, or education. Take the example of religion: any student of comparative doctrines must be struck by the array of similarities among such great religions of the world as Buddhism and Christianity. Despite genuine differences, he cannot help but note the profound values that they cherish in common, even the striking likenesses in their rituals and creeds.

In one sense, accordingly, our span of bridges is more essential to human existence and development than any actual bridge of concrete, steel, or wood. People of all walks of life, from all parts of the earth, from all periods of history, join in perpetual crossings. Many never do cross, of course: ignorance, poverty, slavery, disease, hatred, and fear are among the reasons why only comparatively few have ever left the security of their abodes on the one shore for the insecurities on the other. Yet we must remember that these same factors may also increase the traffic. Hatred has helped to bring about many a bloody conquest of foreign lands. Poverty has forced untold millions to search for real or fanciful lands of opportunity.

At any rate, more people are venturing back and forth today than ever before. Transportation by air enables one to span great oceans in less time than it once took to span a good-sized lake. Communication is much swifter too, so that today you and I can talk across the entire earth almost as easily as we talk across the room. Knowledge, meanwhile, is expanding and spreading at a breathtaking rate. And as it does, more and more people everywhere are eager to learn all they can of the nature of the physical and biological world of the natural sciences; all they can of the human world of the behavioral sciences; all they can of the esthetic world of the painters, sculptors, writers, and musicians; all they can, finally, of the philosophies of their own and other cultures.

And so, in turn, as more and more of us become teachers or other leaders in education, we find ourselves needing to relate more and more effectively all *we* can, too, of the knowledge available from science, art, and philosophy to the daily lives of people—that is, to their immediate experience.

The Bridge of Philosophy

Return now to the central bridge in our model: philosophy. We want to see more specifically what its function is not only in relation to the other two bridges but to the sources and goals of human life that produced the need for bridges in the first place.

Here it is important to observe a difference between the way philosophy is frequently studied today and the way we now wish to study it. Courses taught in college departments of philosophy usually take two or three forms. One form is the history of the subject, although this is more often than not limited to Western philosophy to the neglect of the magnificent thought of the East. Another form is the study of subdivisions of the field—logic, ethics, and esthetics, particularly. (Specialization is prevalent also among present-day philosophers.) Still another form is the study of comparative systems of philosophy, again frequently the Western only.

Philosophies of education, as they are traditionally studied, tend toward this latter form. Students are exposed to so-called systems under such rubrics as idealism, realism, pragmatism, scholasticism, and, now quite often, existentialism and logical positivism. While each student is expected typically to decide for himself which, if any, of these alternatives may suit him best, instructors in the philosophy of education also frequently prefer one to another system and evaluate each according to their personal preference. By and large, the effect of this approach is to leave the student with relatively little opportunity to regard philosophy as more than another subject. Its relations either to other great fields of knowledge, such as the arts, or to the practice of education, such as teaching, are often nebulous at best. One may, indeed, question whether philosophy as it is conventionally studied, either in liberal-arts departments or in schools of education, provide young adults with anything like the kind of perspective and sense of relationship of which we have spoken earlier as imperative to our age.

Granting, of course, that the very notion of usefulness may seem anathema to purists of philosophic lore, how can philosophy become more useful? One answer is suggested again by our multidisciplinary model. Philosophy here is conceived not as a self-contained esoteric discipline aloof from and often indifferent to other disciplines, but as a kind of bridge from and to these others. Thus, to a great extent, it draws its own resources and especially much of its inspiration from the arts and sciences. To an equally great extent, it then applies its interpretations to fields of practice—in our case, to education; in other cases, to medicine, management, law, religion, and to various others. In brief, philosophy as we view it in the context of our interest is primarily an *applied* discipline. The most important test of its significance lies precisely in what difference it makes not only to professional experience but, beyond that, to the problems of everyday life.

What, then, more specifically, is the role philosophy performs in its mediating station between the arts and sciences, on one side, and professional practice, on the other side? It performs a number of important functions and, in the next chapter, we note these with some care. Here, we merely indicate that they are of at least three principal varieties: (1) to examine critically the assumptions that underlie all fields of knowledge and experience; (2) to delineate common denominators both within and among these fields; and (3) to search for and perhaps to discover the goals and purposes that may conceivably govern knowledge and experience.

This is not to suggest that philosophers are fully agreed on the particular methodologies and frameworks through which they perform these major functions. On the contrary, we shall find wide disagreements. Some philosophers, indeed, would doubtless dispute even the legitimacy of all three functions, preferring (with the logical positivists, say) to regard only the first as any longer proper. Nevertheless, though we recognize that different philosophies may utilize them differently, our own approach favors all three functions.

The Bridge of the Arts and Sciences

Philosophy in general, we have said, should draw upon the knowledge and experience of the arts and sciences for much of its own vitality and substance. The philosophy of education should do exactly the same. Insofar as the education of teachers fails to make this kind of knowledge possible, the accusations frequently leveled against it to the effect that it is flimsy, boring, and superficial are altogether justified. The trouble, however, is that the role of the so-called liberal arts taken as a whole is itself far from satisfactory. Specialization and atomization of subject matter, not to mention the sterility of innumerable courses, all mitigate against any kind of assurance that the average liberal-arts graduate is necessarily qualified to enter either upon practical duties or further training in a professional field.

How can we strengthen this assurance? For the profession of education, at any rate, the answer first of all lies in the bridge of philosophy. By connecting what is more relevant in the arts and sciences to what is most relevant in the practice of education, one path has been opened to the needed integration.

Another question logically follows: What then *is* most relevant? Our answer centers in what we now wish to call "explosive ideas." We mean the kind that exert powerful, even revolutionary, influence upon contemporary civilization—ideas that have profoundly changed and continue to change in our generation the immediate experiences of countless individuals, groups, classes, even whole nations. Perhaps the study of such ideas is included, more or less, in standard liberal-arts curricula. Hopefully, even students of education have already been exposed to their importance. Even so, we propose to treat them in a special way—that is, for their remarkable pertinence to the field of education.

But *what* explosive ideas? In the next chapter, we answer this question more fully. They are evident, however, in the subtitle of this book: *Culture, Class, and Evolution.* These ideas are not, of course, the only ones we could select. There are many others. Nevertheless, we shall find them to be excellent symbols of what we mean by *explosive* ideas. We shall find, indeed, that because they make a great deal of difference to human struggles and hopes, they make a great deal of difference, also, to the theory and practice of education.

The Bridge of Educational Practice

The divisions of practice to which we shall give chief attention are: first, curriculum activities and programs; second, learning-teaching experience; third, the control of education. Like our three explosive ideas, they certainly make no claim to exclusiveness. Others doubtless overlap with these, for there are many kinds of practice.

To say much more here about the spheres of practice is not now necessary. Let us reaffirm, however—to return once more to our bridge metaphor—that the traffic is seldom one way. While it is surely true that theory, especially philosophic theory, clarifies practice, we should never forget that the application of philosophy to institutional experience pays rich dividends back into philosophy. In the same way, and here we need to emphasize a point that has not been emphasized sufficiently, it is not enough to assert that the arts and sciences are the principal philosophic resources, for it is also true that philosophy contributes immensely to the arts and sciences in turn. These general statements should become more meaningful in the discussions that follow.

Concluding Comment

What then shall we say is the rationale of this book? Primarily, it is to provide both seasoned and prospective members of the educational profession with a fresh outlook on their impending great responsibilities. Such an outlook is characterized by the term "multidisciplinary." It includes three indispensable bridges of knowledge and experience: (1) explosive ideas from the arts and sciences, (2) philosophies of education, and (3) representative practices of education.

Bridges, however, never exist for their own sake, nor are they constructed merely to reinforce each other. They exist because, by means of them, people are able to reach each other more easily, to communicate more clearly and, above all, to share more fully in the welter of experiences that constitute the ways of human life. The arts, the sciences, philosophy, and education are in this sense ways *to* life as well as ways *of* life. They were created by people, they have been developed for people, and they continue to be the servants of people. In our preoccupation with specialized interests, in our fascination with the lore of philosophy, we sometimes forget what seems to be an obvious truth. This book is intended to help us remember.

2

THE USE OF EXPLOSIVE IDEAS IN EDUCATION

How We Shall Proceed

The bridge-building model previously pictured also provides the plan for our study. The following three sections are organized in essentially the same sequence.

The first chapter of each section considers the nature of the explosive idea itself. Here we attempt to encapsulate the definitions, discoveries, and generalizations that authorities in the given idea tend to agree upon. Because, however, each idea is such a dynamic one, no claim is made that our answer to such a question as "What is culture?" is indisputable. Actually, as in the case of class and evolution, relatively few statements are beyond debate. All we can claim is that, within the severe limits of competence and space, the first chapter in each sequence is as authoritative as we have been able to fashion it.

The second chapter in the three-stage design recalls the bridge of philosophy. Thus our interest here is in such questions as this: What does a respective idea mean when its assumptions are critically analyzed by philosophic specialists? We do not necessarily say that only professional philosophers are competent in this kind of skill. Scholars in the particular field of the explosive idea—a few outstanding biologists would be an example in the case of evolution—are very much concerned not only with critical examination of the assumptions of their field, but with other philosophic problems, such as, say, the "purposes," if any, of the evolutionary process.

The third sequential chapter in each section focuses upon certain applications of the explosive idea to education itself—now perceived, however, through the prisms of philosophy. As in the case of the two preceding chapters, this one is unavoidably selective. The few applications presented for purposes of illustration aim to encourage readers to go further with applications of their own. Insofar as each third chapter is successful, it demonstrates how professional education becomes dependent upon basic knowledge from other sources *than* education. At the same time it tests the nature of such knowledge in the laboratories of practice. Thus, it may contribute "feedback" effects of substantial value—that is, counterinfluences both upon the nature of the respective idea and upon its philosophic meanings.

Anticipating the Explosive Ideas

Culture, class, and evolution, to reiterate, are intended to exemplify and dramatize the multidisciplinary approach to professional education. By no means are they the only powerful ideas among all the great ones available for comparable treatment. Why, then, are they selected?

In the first place, quite frankly, they have fascinated the author for a long time. Hence, it is understandable that they would be preferred to ideas in which he is less interested and certainly less informed. Another author might utilize exactly the same model and draw upon, let us say, the idea of *self* as it has recently developed in the psychological sciences, upon the idea of *creativity* in the field of arts, upon the idea of *energy* in the physical sciences, or upon a number of others.

In the second place, the ideas we have chosen nevertheless do have immense relevance for every individual who plans to enter the field of education. Let us go still further and insist that the three we consider are indispensable to professional competence and responsibility. No classroom teacher on any level (from nursery school to college), no principal or superintendent, no supervisor, no guidance officer—in short, no member of the educational profession—can rightly claim that he is fully qualified to serve until and unless he is prepared to recognize the pervasive influence of culture, the power of class, and the forces of evolution that affect, directly as well as indirectly, virtually every phase of educational activity. The sections before us aim to support this strong assertion.

Let us for another moment glance at the three ideas taken together. In their modern form, all three are something like one century old. Of course, their origins are much older, going back at least as far as the ancient Greeks; of course, too, they are constantly being modified today. Nevertheless, it was in about the middle third of the nineteenth century that they achieved sufficient crystallization in modern form to begin to affect radically the beliefs and actions of vast numbers of individuals, groups, and institutions.

Moreover, with each of these ideas we often associate both a famous name and a particular date. With evolution we think, of course, of Charles Darwin. The key year is 1859, when the first edition of *The Origin of Species* was presented to the public. With class, the name of Karl Marx is most likely to occur to us. The year we might choose is 1848 when, collaborating with Friedrich Engels, he issued, the earthshaking *Communist Manifesto*. Although culture is not quite so conspicuously identified with an outstanding figure, many scholars would undoubtedly select Edward B. Tylor, sometimes called the father of scientific anthropology, whose pioneering work, *Primitive Culture*, appeared originally in 1871.

All three ideas, we further observe, are central to the social sciences. Culture is the master concept of anthropology. Class is usually associated with sociology, although economics and political science could make a strong claim too. Evolution differs from the other two in the respect that its original scientific focus was biological rather than sociological. Yet we shall find it to be profoundly involved not only with the social sciences but with other natural sciences such as astronomy. We place our study of evolution third in the order of treatment deliberately: not only does it embrace in some ways both of the other ideas, but it provides us with a modern view of the world as a whole—indeed, with one kind of intriguing philosophy of education that, at the same time, is thoroughly multidisciplinary.

The Functions of Philosophy

Here we begin to look a little more carefully at the functions of philosophy—our purpose being to prepare for their bridge-building tasks.

The discipline of philosophy is often subdivided into three principal branches. One, *epistemology*, is concerned with examining and establishing criteria of reliable knowledge. A second, *ontology* (sometimes defined synonymously with *metaphysics*), tries to discover criteria of reality. A third, *axiology*, searches for criteria of value.

Roughly, the functions of philosophy touched upon in Chapter 1 overlap with these three branches. Epistemology is especially interested in criticizing the assumptions by which we regard some statements as true, others false, and therefore some knowledge as genuine knowledge, other kinds not. (Logic, the methodology of accurate thinking, may be regarded as a further subdivision of epistemology.) Ontology is interested in the nature of the real world as against imaginary or fictitious portrayals; thus, it is interested in such questions as whether reality is in some sense one—that is, whether it possesses any common character that is always and everywhere real—or whether it is always a plurality of real things and events. Axiology, because its interest centers in the meaning and existence of values, constantly raises such questions as whether or not life is purposeful. But it is not concerned merely with the kind of values associated with good or bad conduct, or with right or wrong purposes; it is also concerned with values that establish whether a given work of art is beautiful or ugly—that is, with esthetic values.

In the applied discipline of educational philosophy, let us regard epistemology, ontology, and axiology as tools that enable educators to accomplish two principal tasks. On the one hand, they interpret philosophically the resources of the arts and sciences available and essential to education. On the other hand, they provide more depth, consistency, and direction to the work of education by means of these resources.

We shall later show frequent examples of how both tasks are performed. Meanwhile, however, because our statements thus far are necessarily abstract, let us consider one or two examples. Certain critics of American education (Paul Goodman, in *Growing Up Absurd* and other books, is an excellent case in point) argue persuasively that schools and colleges often seem to be engaged in a more or less unconscious conspiracy: to prevent students from discovering the truth about the real world in which they actually live. Although such accusations sometimes seem extreme, they are by no means unconvincing. Thus, to what extent do children in the South obtain unbiased knowledge of the Negro problem? To what extent do children anywhere in America obtain a picture of economic and political events not colored by the propaganda or vested interests of some official or unofficial pressure group? To what extent, also, do they have opportunity to consider under critical and responsible educational direction the changing mores of our age—especially the values of sexual morality?

Please note how, merely by asking these questions, all three branches of philosophy begin to operate. Note also how the questions overlap. Thus, what is true or false about the Negro problem depends obviously upon what is real or illusory about the situation of the Negro people. Similarly, what is good or bad about sexual experience is closely related to both its reality and truth. The branches of philosophy, while to some extent they can be kept quite separate and treated separately, often interpenetrate.

Equally important, we need to observe how in these illustrations our philosophic tools work back and forth from educational practice to the disciplines of knowledge from which education draws. The question of the Negro problem once more affords an apt illustration. What the schools teach or do about this question surely depends upon the *reliability* of their resources—resources that must therefore derive, certainly not from the opinions and prejudices of lay citizens, but from the sciences of society and race. The moment that we speak of reliability, however, we must assume criteria of knowledge that *are* reliable. Hence, we are once more faced with epistemological questions that some scientists of race and culture have considered carefully. Yet, if they happen to be practicing researchers impatient with theoretical preoccupations, they may not have considered them carefully at all.

We wish to emphasize that the functions of philosophy, although at times they must surely seem distant from down-to-earth practice, are by no means necessarily as distant as some academic philosophers try their best to make them appear. Certainly, they are not when they become, as the philosophy of education properly becomes, a discipline concerned to apply its special facilities to the problems of everyday educational experience.

Types of Educational Philosophy

Each of the three branches of philosophy—the theories, respectively, of knowledge, reality, and value—function in many varieties of philosophic systems. *Idealists*, for example, are idealistic ontologists—that is, they discover the principles of reality in their conception of the universe as spiritual or mental in substance. *Materialists* are materialistic axiologists—that is, they find the meaning of value in material events such as economic patterns. *Pragmatists* are pragmatic epistemologists—that is, truths are determined by their practical workability in ongoing experience.

We have already hinted at the inadequacy of such traditional categories. Too often, moreover, they are approached as more or less self-sufficient systems of thought. While, certainly, the history of philosophy continues to be an indispensable resource, and while these and other types of philosophy rightly continue to exert substantial influence, we wish to suggest an alternative approach that is, at the same time, congenial to our bridge-building model. This approach relates effectively both to the three ideas selected from the social sciences and to the sphere of practice.

Let us call our own preferred types by the following four terms, all of them being familiar to many American philosophers of education: *essentialism, progressivism, perennialism,* and *reconstructionism.* In the briefest possible terms, what does each mean?

Essentialism may be defined as a philosophy of education centering in the belief that schools should be dedicated primarily to basic learning of the essential principles, laws, customs, and skills of the established social order. To be sure, it recognizes at times the need of limited social change. Nevertheless, its primary emphasis is not on change but on social stability. Epistemologically, truth is determined by the exactitude with which the essentials of tested knowledge are conveyed by the teacher to the mind of the learner. Axiologically, the primary values that should be taught through education are those most firmly established in the course of the modern centuries of Western civilization. Ontologically, essentialists may hold different conceptions of reality—some contending that it is spiritual (these are idealistic essentialists); others, that it is objectively real in the sense of being primarily physical or material (these are realistic essentialists). Whichever their ontology, however, essentialists still regard education as primarily an agency for the transmission of the world of law and objective order.

Progressivism, while agreeing with essentialists that education rightly plays a transmitting role, is much more inclined to regard it as a way of modifying the patterns of human life. There is, moreover, one crucially important methodology by which the modifying process takes place in education. This is called the experimental method of inquiry. Above all, progressivism is interested in teaching the student how to think and act as scientists think and act when they are attacking and solving problems. This philosophy of education is grounded in the epistemology, axiology, and ontology of pragmatism—sometimes called instrumentalism or experimentalism. Truths are the products of scientific problem solving. Values are shaped effectively by the same process. Reality is defined as continuous experience with and of natural events. Education's principal business is to enable young people to progress by learning how to grow—that is, by sharing directly, actively, and intelligently in this kind of reality.

Perennialism, the oldest historically of the four outlooks, is perhaps most simply approached by recalling how a botanist classifies a perennial plant. It is, of course, one that renews itself each season without reseeding; thus, it is sometimes referred to as an "everlasting" plant. Comparably, the perennialist in education is interested above all in discovering, teaching, and learning those principles of reality, truth, and value that have the same everlasting qualities of the permanent, unchanging, and timeless. These principles are not at all easy to come by, however. They require mental discipline of a high order and rigorous cultivation of the intellectual faculties, including intuition. Thus, while every citizen should be educated up to the limit of his capacities, it is only in the higher learning and only among the highly qualified that we may expect perennialist education to function at its best. On lower levels, education is more properly concerned with the transmitting roles that essentialism emphasizes.

Reconstruction is often linked with progressivism, just as perennialism may be linked with essentialism. And while it is not improper to speak therefore of two *pairs* of philosophies, one finds also significant differences among all four. Reconstructionism, for example, is more goal-centered than progressivism—that is, more concerned with the ends and purposes of civilization than is the more process-oriented experimental approach of progressivist educators. This does not mean that reconstructionists do not also utilize the experimental approach, for they constantly do. Yet even here one detects varying emphases: the methodologies in which they are interested most centrally are those of group involvement and social action because these, they contend, are likely to be most frequently neglected by other philosophies of education, even by the many progressivists who seem to be chiefly interested in the growth of the child. What reconstructionists desire most is the kind of education that will engage directly in the rebuilding of culture on a world scale, for they hold that we are now deep in a period of history that can otherwise easily lead to complete disintegration.

It becomes necessary now to register several qualifications. First, each of these philosophies of education is vastly more complex and subtle than any abbreviated statement can possibly suggest. Second, each borrows from the others and contributes so much to the others that it is well to think of them functioning on a continuum; they are definitely *not* completely separable theories. Third, they could not for a moment claim to encompass all varieties of contemporary thought: other theories (existentialism is one) exert a good deal of influence that our four positions only partially appreciate. Finally, none is to be regarded as a "system" that has any kind of autonomous, self-contained existence of its own. All of them, rather, are nothing more nor less than perspectives upon a diffused, not to say confused, cultural-educational landscape. This final point is of particular significance in terms of our bridge-building model: each philosophy must be interpreted in relation, on the one hand, to the resources of art and science from which it is largely derived and upon which it retroacts and, on the other hand, to its effects upon the concrete work of education. In the context of this book, philosophies of education are never theories for the sake of theories as such. They are, please recall, applied philosophies.

The Sphere of Practice

Each of the following three sections concludes with a chapter of application to educational problems and activities. The practices selected—*curriculum, learning-teaching,* and *control*—are obvious enough at first glance. Yet, at second glance they prove to be anything but obvious.

Even the term "curriculum" is open to various definitions. While we often think of it as a structure of courses, experts in the field may regard it not only in this traditional way but also in terms of broad fields, cores, units, and other integrating concepts that cut across subject-matter lines. Gordon Mackenzie, an authority, defines it in an even more comprehensive way: the curriculum is "the learner's engagements with various aspects of the environment which have been planned under the direction of the school." The term "engagement," in turn, "is used to mean what the learner meets face-to-face, what he attends to, or what he is involved in. . . . It suggests more than mere activity. Obviously there can be engagements with teachers, classmates, or others; with physical factors such as materials and facilities; and with subject matter, ideas, or symbols."* We shall assume Mackenzie's broad conception in our later comments on curriculum practice.

Learning-teaching is a reciprocal process, for each typically requires the other. Like the term "curriculum," learning is by no means simple, as any serious student of educational psychology discovers for himself. The several major theories of learning have their own enthusiastic advocates, and some of these theories are being constantly subjected to experimental testing. The one precaution that can be stressed here is to avoid at all costs the "commonsense" view that the only valid test of learning is "mastery" of subject matter mandated by the school Actually, of course, such mastery is at best only one kind of learning. To mention one other that will interest us again: *concomitant learning* is the sort that occurs through direct association with people— usually through informally rather than formally planned experiences. Yet, it may often prove more powerful in its effects on the learner than typically structured kinds.

Teaching is equally a term of complex meanings. It depends at least in considerable part upon what the teacher conceives to be

*Gordon Mackenzie, in Mathew B. Miles (ed.), *Innovation in Education* (New York: Bureau of Publications, Teachers College, Columbia University, 1964), p. 402.

the learning process that he or she is supposed to direct. One widely held view of teaching that we must be wary of is to identify it with *indoctrination*. True enough, much teaching is exactly that—namely, the imposition of a particular doctrine or set of beliefs upon children who are then expected to accept what is taught as the inviolable truth. Other experts in teaching, however, regard teaching and indoctrination as completely antithetical: for them teaching is rather a way to develop the habit of critical awareness toward every kind of doctrine.

The concept of control involves such issues as these: Who shall determine the policies of education? How shall they be determined? Who shall carry them out? Like other concepts of practice, control too is difficult to define. The easy answer, to be sure, is that school boards must determine policies, and superintendents must carry them out. But this is much *too* easy. Should not teachers and even students also have a voice? And what about the state and federal governments? One quickly discovers, indeed, that the moment the concept of control is carefully considered, basic issues of political philosophy come to the fore. Witness as instances the sweeping decisions of the Supreme Court on racial segregation and religious indoctrination in the public schools.

Thus, whether we are considering problems of the curriculum, of learning, or of control, we are soon considering problems also in educational philosophy—problems, moreover, about which the four types that we have epitomized above often provide quite opposed solutions. At the same time, we are drawn back to the sources from which they arise—that is, to the arts and sciences and then, eventually, to the immediate experiences of human life that are their fountainhead.

The Need for Supplementation

As we turn next to culture, the first of our major ideas, one recommendation to the student becomes paramount. This is to supplement the present chapter and those we now confront with substantial reading in the sources upon which all of them depend. With the perennialist philosophers of education, we believe that anything but superficial understanding of ideas as important as these is utterly impossible unless one comes directly into contact both with their original creators and their chief interpretors. The bibliography provided for this purpose is not an extensive one, but it is chosen with care and the expectation that it will be utilized.

There is another reason, besides the need to become familiar with basic resources, why we urge that the bibliography be drawn upon abundantly. This book does not pretend to interpret the great ideas dispassionately or neutrally. While it is hoped that the first of the sequence of three chapters in each section is reasonably objective, the second and third often reveal frank preferences for one philosophic or educational interpretation as against another. The opportunities for further reading provide comparisons of such preferences with those of other writers.

It is always the reader's privilege to agree or disagree with the author's own judgments. It is not his privilege either to accept or reject these judgments without fairly considering them in the light of the further evidence and authority that the bibliography provides.

Recommended Readings for Chapter 2

Berelson, Bernard, and Steiner, Gary A., *Human Behavior: An Inventory of Scientific Findings*. New York: Harcourt, Brace & World, 1964. (Overview of the behavioral sciences.)

Brameld, Theodore, *Toward a Reconstructed Philosophy of Education*. New York: Holt, Rinehart & Winston, 1956; *Education for the Emerging Age*. New York: Harper & Row, 1965. (Reconstructionist view.)

Brennan, Joseph G., *The Meaning of Philosophy*. New York: Harper & Row, 1953. (Introduction.)

Brubacher, John, *Modern Philosophies of Education*. 3d ed. revised. New York: McGraw-Hill, 1962.

Council for Basic Education, *The Case for Basic Education*. Boston: Little, Brown, 1959. (Essentialist approach.)

Dewey, John, *Democracy and Education*. New York: Macmillan, 1916. (Progressivist classic.)

Goodman, Paul, *Growing Up Absurd*. New York: Random House, 1960.

Hutchins, Robert M., *The Conflict in Education*. New York: Harper & Row, 1953. (Perennialist view.)

Kilpatrick, William H., *Philosophy of Education*. New York: Macmillan, 1951. (Progressivist view.)

Mackenzie, Gordon, in Miles, Mathew B. (ed.), *Innovation in Education*, New York: Bureau of Publications, Teachers College, Columbia University, 1964.

Maritain, Jacques, *Education at the Crossroads*. New Haven: Yale University Press, 1943. (Perennialist classic.)

Montague, William P., *The Ways of Knowing*. London: Allen & Unwin, 1925. (Epistemologies.)

Morris, Van Cleve, *Philosophy and the American School*. Boston: Houghton Mifflin, 1961. (Overview of contemporary theories.)

Phenix, Philip H., *Education and the Common Good*. New York: Harper & Row, 1961. (Implicitly essentialist.); (ed.), *Philosophies of Education*. New York: Wiley, 1961. (Television transcripts of representative views in educational philosophy.)

Prosch, Harry. *The Genesis of Twentieth Century Philosophy*. New York: Doubleday, 1964. (History.)

Rader, Melvin, *Ethics and the Human Community*. New York: Holt, Rinehart & Winston, 1964. (Axiologies.)

Whitehead, Alfred N., *Science and the Modern World*. New York: Macmillan, 1925. (Ontological classic.)

II

THE EXPLOSIVE IDEA

OF CULTURE

3

WHAT IS CULTURE?

Tylor's Definition and Its Implications

The most famous definition of culture was published in 1871 by that giant figure in the history of anthropology, Edward B. Tylor, who was mentioned in Chapter 2. "Culture," he said, "is that complex whole which includes knowledge, belief, art, morals, custom, and any other capabilities and habits acquired by man as a member of society."* This is not the only definition, of course, but anthropologists, the scientists of culture, are agreed that it is a very good one. Let us dissect it into five important components: belief, morals, acquired, complex whole, and society.

Start with the last component. Culture occurs when man is a member of "society." Sometimes anthropologists, speaking loosely, use the words "society" and "culture" as synonyms, but they should not. Society is often regarded by the scientists of society, the sociologists, simply as an organized group. Therefore, it does not necessarily involve any of the other characteristics in Tylor's definition. The distinction between culture and society is easily understood when we recall that many animals—from bees and ants to elephants—live in organized groups, some of them very highly organized. But these societies are inherited through the genes. Bees, as we know, are not taught how to build their wonderful social structures—they do it by what we often call

*Edward B. Tylor, *Primitive Culture* (5th ed.; London: S. Murray, 1929), p. 1.

instinct, generation after generation, without perceptible change. The capacity to build societies may be inherited genetically by human beings as well.

The distinction between society and culture is perhaps not as simple as we have made it appear on the side of nonhuman animals. Some students of, for example, beaver colonies contend that they possess features that seem to be cultural or pseudocultural. Nevertheless, if it remains true that countless societies do not have cultures, it is even more true that no cultures lack societies. All cultures are organized into groups that are more or less efficient and systematic in the way their members relate to one another. This is the social aspect of culture.

What does a culture have that a society does not? This leads us to the other components selected from Tylor's definition. One of the most important is "belief." Societies of nonhuman animals are not characterized by the beliefs of their members, but societies of human beings are. All human groups possess sets of beliefs that are fundamental to their ways of life. One could even argue that the single most distinctive feature of culture as compared to society is that the former is governed by patterns of belief while the latter is not. If we define philosophy in a simple way as an expression of beliefs, then it follows that there has never been a culture known to students that has not possessed a philosophy—an assertion supported by Paul Radin's remarkable book, *Primitive Man as Philosopher*, in which he demonstrates that even cultures without written language have elaborate patterns of belief. Clyde Kluckhohn, a leading authority on the Navajo Indian culture of the Southwestern region of the United States, also showed conclusively how subtly and comprehensively this indigenous American culture has formulated its beliefs about moral conduct, about the universe, about political obligations, and about every important phase of its way of life.

Take a third term from the definition: "complex whole." Here again the difference from society is striking. Some societies have very complex structures, but some do not. A single family of bears, for example, is a simple group with only meager organization. But all cultures are much more complex than that—even those of nomadic families and tribes.

Here we come to one of the most important dimensions of culture—that of order. For our purpose, the order of culture, viewed generally, is always a complex whole. To be sure, the degree of complexity varies enormously. By comparison with the Australian aborigines, for example, the culture of New England is very complex indeed—so much so that anthropologists have thus far usually preferred to concentrate on simpler cultures even though these, too, require lifetimes of study. Also, one must keep in mind that the order of any culture really consists of *orders*. Sometimes these, in turn, lead us to perceive subcultures—that is, cultures within a culture. A university has many characteristics of a subculture, one of these being its own types of order— or disorder!—ranging all the way from the structure of a single classroom to the administrative system of control. In turn, the order of a university is part of the wider order of the community, the state, the region, the nation, and, finally, the most complex whole of all: world order.

Another crucial component of our definition is the term "acquired." Looking back at the definition, one notes just two verbs: the verb "include," which is important because it points up the vast inclusiveness of cultural order; the other, the verb "acquire." The term "acquire" suggests, for one thing, that culture is the product of action. To acquire something assumes some kind of effort whether we acquire property, or acquire a wife, or acquire knowledge. Sometimes a great deal of effort is expended over a long period of time, as in acquiring by force or exploration the whole of a foreign territory.

Thus, the broad concept of cultural process may be suggested by acquiring. Culture not only possesses order, it also possesses process, the most important expression of which may center in the ability to acquire. This ability, we shall see, is complex indeed and also involves the ability to inquire.

The difference between culture and society is graphically demonstrated here when we consider the difference between the way human animals acquire culture and the way other animals do so. Horses, for example, may have simple family societies that they perpetuate through instinct. But they become beasts of burden only when men train them to haul wagons or carry riders. While horses in this sense acquire culture and are members of culture, they cannot train their colts to become beasts of burden. Nor is the knowledge that horses are useful to economic production something that they remember to pass on to successive generations of horses. But men do remember and so perpetuate the process of training horses.

Indeed, the key process of acquiring culture is that of learning and then transmitting and modifying what is learned. Perhaps the commonest example is still the best one—that of learning a language. Everyone knows that when a child acquires fluency in Danish, Chinese, Italian, Russian, or German he literally learns that ability; he does not inherit it. All that he inherits is his larynx and a brain structure complicated enough to develop symbols and to manipulate their sounds through the larynx. But the particular combinations of sound that come out are not inherited; they are entirely acquired. Had you or I been born in China, we would be speaking and reading Chinese with the same fluency that we now speak and write English.

This is one of the marvelous things about the human animal— that he can assure the continuity of culture by acquiring such a process as speaking a language and passing on what he thus acquires from one generation to the next. Think what this means for the term "knowledge" in Tylor's definition: knowledge is a product of the acquiring process of culture—no doubt the most important of all products.

The final term selected from this remarkable sentence is "morals." Every culture has rules of conduct considered by its members to be good or bad, right or wrong. Beyond this, the term "morals" implies that culture is concerned with values— values in the sense that everywhere the order and process of culture possess some kind of worth, some kind of purpose, some kind of standard of what ought to be achieved because it is good and right. These standards may be embodied, to be sure, in art and custom, both of which Tylor also includes in his definition, so that perhaps we can adopt the term "goals" to encompass all kinds of values—moral, esthetic, customary, and others. Thus cultures are, in a profound sense, goal-directed at the same time that they are complex wholes and complex ways of acquiring. This is not to forget that cultures also differ widely in their goals: the problem remains as to whether it is ever legitimate to think of culturally universal values or whether all values are only relative to each particular culture.

Thus far we have selected five terms from Tylor's stimulating definition: society, belief, complex whole, acquired, and morals. We now examine three of them in a somewhat wider context: the term "complex whole," which points to the *order* of culture; the term "acquiring," which points to the *process* of culture; and the term "morals," which points (with the help of art and custom) to the *goals* of culture. Let us state a general proposition. Wherever you view it—on a worldwide scale or in a small community or even as one family—every culture consists of three interrelated dimensions: order, process, and goals. It is impossible to think of any culture without all three.

One may, however, select one or the other of the three dimensions for analytical attention. In doing this, we always artificialize. For instance, if for the moment we concentrate upon order we thrust the concept of process and the concept of goals into the background. This is a perfectly legitimate approach to any complex idea, just as it is to a phenomenon of nature. Consider what happens in a laboratory. When a physiologist dissects a rabbit, he selects, let us say, the skeleton or the nervous system, removes it, and then examines it separately. But the rabbit hardly consists of a nervous system or skeleton alone. The rabbit is a whole organism and, if it is to live, all its parts have to function together. And yet a physiologist may properly separate one part of the rabbit and study that part. This is what we now intend to do with culture—to dissect it. First we examine its order, ignoring for the moment its process and goals.

The Order of Culture

Anthropologists develop various models in looking at the order of a culture. The term "model" is already familiar to us from the first chapter, where we presented one in the form of bridges across a river. In studying culture, we also create models—all of them artificial but nevertheless useful in helping us to visualize what is actually not often visible.

Cultures may be constructed, first of all, in terms of *spatial* models. Suppose we were to fly above a city like Boston and look down. We would see a kind of flat surface of crisscrossing lines that we recognize as streets, interspersed with green areas (parks), blue areas (ponds), and other irregularities. The total effect is that of a complex whole that we view, as it were, "horizontally" from above.

So, too, when an anthropologist tries to construct a spatial model of culture, he may begin with a series of concentric circles. In the center is the order of the family—the nuclear family, as it is sometimes called. Around this is a circle of families joined together in a community. Around the community circle is, perhaps, that of a region or area consisting of a number of communities in the way that Boston is involved in the region of New England. Then another circle may encompass several regions, so that we think of the whole culture of the United States. Finally, we reach the widest order of all: world order, a "family" of nations.

World order is the most comprehensive of all the complex wholes that man has thus far imagined where culture is concerned. In many ways, we may rightfully wonder whether this dimension should be included in our horizontal model, since it is more of a future possibility than a present fact. Yet we are in the process of building one through the United Nations, are we not? At least the glimmerings of world order are clearly discernible. In this example, we cannot, of course, avoid the concept of goals, for a strong United Nations is an order toward which increasing numbers of us wish to move.

But this simple spatial model is incomplete until we recognize that the widening circles are not in fact merely horizontal. Cultures are "vertical," too, in that their orders extend up and down as well as sidewise. If we think of our model now as a kind of elaborate cake, we at once perceive that cultures consist of layers or strata—of people living above and below one another—and we can view their differing habits, beliefs, arts, morals, and practices only by slicing the cake. It symbolizes the fact that people live on different levels according to their prestige, income, kinship patterns, class status. Needless to say, we anticipate here our second explosive idea, that of class. All cultures, even simple ones, seem to have some type of class structure. The main point, however, is that the vertical model helps us to discern the spatial relations of culture in the three standard dimensions of height, width, and depth.

But now, another indispensable feature of cultural order must be introduced: the *temporal*. The artificiality of our dissection is revealed by the static nature of any merely spatial model. One may look down upon Boston from an airplane and not think for the moment of its past or future. There it is—*now*. But, actually, Boston as an American subculture has a fascinating history, too. A physicist might say that it is in a "space-time continuum"—that it is not three-dimensional, after all, but four-dimensional. Culture, in short, has a past, present, and future as well as a horizontal and vertical structure. No culture ever stays put. It is always moving in time. It will never be the same tomorrow as it was yesterday or is today. True, some cultures move much more rapidly than others, one of the unique and dangerous and wonderful things about our own culture being the unbelievable speed of its changes as it accelerates from decade to decade, even month to month. The events that have occurred in the span of life of any reader of this book are so breathtaking that no one can fully comprehend their significance—what they may mean for the good or evil of humanity even in the decades immediately before us.

Another powerful idea anticipated here is, of course, that of evolution. As we shall see, all cultures evolve through time in some form or other, although anthropologists argue with one another about exactly what evolution means to the temporal order of culture.

To summarize our comments about the order of culture, we may think of it as the encompassing spatial-temporal pattern of human relationship—a pattern ranging all the way from the simplest kind of order, that of the family, to the most complex kind, that of a family of nations—a world order still on the horizon of our imaginations.

The Process of Culture

The second dimension of our cultural model, that of process, has been anticipated by virtue of the fact that all cultures change in time. Process is really the aspect concerned with the dynamics of cultural change.

Let us try to exemplify this contention by recalling an earlier one—that the central process of culture is acquiring. Anthropologists often use the term *enculturation* to characterize this process. A child becomes enculturated as he gradually acquires the beliefs, morals, habits, and other characteristics of the culture into which he is born, and as he then adapts and modifies them to suit the changing space-time continuum of his own cultural experience.

Enculturation, however, is manifested in a number of more specific processes, one of the most important being *acculturation*— the process by which members of one culture acquire some of the characteristics of another culture through contact—usually direct continuous contact over a fairly long period of time. Consider our own American culture: we are, perhaps, the most wonderful example in all history of what happens when cultures come into prolonged contact—in our case, of course, dozens of cultures. No wonder that we have been called the "melting pot" nation. In hundreds of college classrooms even in this period when migration has tapered off, one can easily discover students whose parents or grandparents came from some distant part of the world. Each of these new residents brought with him as a large part of his invisible baggage the cultural traits of his own culture. Many such traits were in turn incorporated into the life of the new culture. At the same time they were, of course, modified in the process: rarely did the American culture acquire them without also relating them to others already here or brought by still other people from still other cultures.

Also fundamental is the process of *assimiliation*. When acculturation continues so long and so persistently that you can no longer distinguish one culture, or even some phase of that culture, from another, then we say that assimilation has occurred. Looking down once more from our airplane, we know if we have any familiarity with Boston that both acculturation and assimilation still go on. Bostonians whose ancestors came to America in the eighteenth century are more assimilated than many Irish-Americans or Italian-Americans, although one also finds in both these groups examples of fairly complete assimilation. In speech, for example, the younger generation of Irish-Americans have lost so much of the brogue of their grandparents that only an expert might detect their original culture by listening to them. Yet, in some of their customs and values they are by no means completely assimilated. As a matter of fact, Irish-Americans have made a deep acculturative impress upon the remainder of the Boston subculture through their political acumen and the power of their religious organizations.

Such processes as acculturation and assimilation—they are not, of course, the only processes of enculturation—should not be thought of exclusively as smooth easy ways of acquiring cultural traits. In some cases they occur almost unconsciously—in speech habits, say. But often the processes of culture generate tensions and even upheavals of a quite literal kind. One example very much before us in current years is the situation in Africa. Why has there been so much unrest on that great continent? Part of the reason, surely, is the boomerang effect called *nativism*—a process resulting from the attempt of one culture to impose itself too rapidly upon another culture. Especially in South Africa, the nativist reaction to foreign culture is one of resistance, hostility, and violence. So it is important to stress that the basic process of acquiring is not always a pretty thing; sometimes it is cruel and ruthless. One of the great problems the world faces today is how to effect such processes as acculturation not with violence but with peaceful benefit to all the cultures that inevitably find themselves in direct and increasing contact.

Nevertheless, because acquiring is often overt, even violent, learning viewed culturally is equally so. Of great importance to teachers is the realization that one becomes encultured by no means merely in a verbal or intellectual way, but viscerally, muscularly, emotionally. One acquires the habits of cultural membership not in the mind alone, but in habits of action and practice. The full significance of this realization, as we hope to reemphasize in Chapter 5, is that enculturation embraces a process far wider than the merely intellectual.

Here the term "concomitant learning" may be recalled. It means any kind of learning that occurs in feelings and attitudes through exposure to such pervasive cultural experience as prejudices and hatreds and loves. Education must take this wider process into full consideration if it is to benefit by the inclusive meaning of enculturation.

The Goals of Culture

The third dimension of culture—goals—may be clarified by selecting two problems for brief consideration. Both of them are just as important to the teacher as they are to the anthropologist, although thus far they are rarely recognized as such.

The first problem is whether every culture has its own unique goals that belong to it alone, or whether there are some goals that cut across and are common to many cultures. Here is the cultural version of the old problem of *relative and universal values*.

The issue is beautifully and dramatically treated in James

Michener's novel *Hawaii*. In the first part, he describes how the Polynesians migrated to Hawaii more than a thousand years ago, carrying with them their own religion, their own family structure and government, their own ways of acquiring. Whether or not his novel is ethnologically accurate at every point, its effect is one of deep sympathy and admiration for the values—moral and esthetic—of this primitive people. The gods that they worshiped, for example, had profound worth for them—worth that commands one's respect even if one's own gods are different from theirs.

Now this is the view of cultural relativism. The relativist is one who says we must evaluate every culture by its own goals and not by our goals. If we judge the morals of the indigenous Hawaiian culture by our values, we commit the *fallacy of ethnocentrism*— of assuming that all ethnic groups should be praised or blamed according to whether they reflect our own central values.

When, in the novel, missionaries from America go to Hawaii to convert the heathen, Michener is scathing in his portrayal of their ethnocentricism—of their righteous air of superiority. But he also portrays certain of his characters otherwise—as attempting to understand the goals of the natives and to discover similarities among their goals and those of the American, Chinese, and other cultural groups who migrated to Hawaii.

The issue is sharpened when we ask: What shall our attitude be toward, say, the values of a culture that practiced polygamy? Both the native Hawaiians and migrant Chinese did practice polygamy, but the Americans did not.

At least three alternative answers are possible. One is for us simply to agree with the American missionaries and thus to reveal our own ethnocentric values. A second is to declare that polygamy is all right "for them" but monogamy all right "for us." A third answer is to suggest that one may discover a value called human love—a value that pervades all cultures on earth, a value far deeper than such particular customs as polygamy, monogamy, and polyandry through which love is institutionalized. This third alternative—the love of a man and woman, or even of more than one man or woman for each other—is a universal value, while the many ways in which cultures sanction the sex relationship with or without marriage implies relativistic values.

One of the perplexing questions that our kind of world faces is whether there are universal values in any scientifically demonstrable sense. This is not merely an academic question. Upon its answer may rest the future of mankind itself. For unless the goal of world order is grounded in profoundly common attributes, there is little chance of its success.

The other question we have selected to highlight the meaning of cultural goals follows closely upon the question of relativism and universalism. Anthropologists do not help us as much here as do philosophers. Suppose, as some anthropologists already hold, that we can discover a group of universal values in the sense that they are shared by cultures everywhere on earth—love being one, cooperation being, perhaps, another. (Actually, a number of students of this question agree that we know more about universal *dis*values or negative values, such as murder or incest, than we do about positive ones.) In any case, does it follow from the *fact* of any universal values that they are also necessarily *desirable*—that they are worth believing in? That is to say, is it not one thing to describe values scientifically, as anthropologists try to do, but quite another thing to show that these values are worth committing ourselves to—that they are goals we can wholeheartedly fight for?

The point may be made in another way. Suppose we agree that there is a sense in which "all men are brothers" and, hence, that brotherhood is a kind of universal value. But how desirable is it really? The test of its desirability lies in whether we in the United States, for example, would be willing to join with people of other nations in a common form of political organization where traditional relativistic values are, at least in part, abrogated in favor of the universal value of world citizenship. It is not lip service to such a value that is the test; it is whether we believe it to be important enough to justify subordination of our own interests, with the inevitable consequence of limiting the national sovereignty of the United States (or any other member country) in favor of clear international sovereignty. The dimension of cultural goals involves, therefore, not only a description of what these goals are, but the normative questions of what they ought to be.

Here, the relation of this dimension to that of process and order also becomes crucial. The goals of any culture help to select the process or processes that are needed to reach them: how a culture acts always depends in an important part upon what it aims to achieve. Similarly, the kinds of order established by a culture are shaped by what its values condone: the class structure illustrates well the American moral attitude toward the positions of status that it tacitly approves—for example, the approval that our culture frequently extends to men who have achieved success in business enterprise. Such approval does not, however, necessarily carry with it any clear justification that can be formulated axiologically; thus here again we are faced with the question of what kinds of cultural order are desirable. Or, in the language of Chapter 2, what are the axiological criteria that are presupposed in the values of business success?

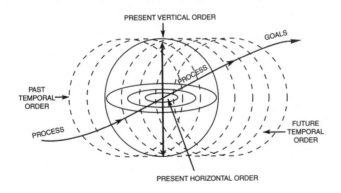

Conclusion

In this chapter we have tried to answer the question "What is culture?" by spelling out some important implications in Tylor's famous definition. It should be noted that his is not necessarily the best possible definition. Some characteristics are undoubtedly left out. Nevertheless, by means of this definition we have been able to focus upon three fundamental aspects of culture, all interrelated. The diagram on the previous page may help to visualize the main points of our discussion.

Recommended Readings for Chapter 3

Brameld, Theodore, *Cultural Foundations of Education: An Interdisciplinary Exploration*. New York: Harper & Row, 1957.

Honigmann, John, *Understanding Culture*. New York: Harper & Row, 1963. (Introduction to anthropology.)

Kluckhohn, Clyde, *Mirror for Man*. New York: McGraw-Hill, 1949. (Introduction to anthropology.)

Kroeber, Alfred L., *Anthropology*. New York: Harcourt, Brace & World, 1948.

Kroeber, Alfred L., and Kluckhohn, Clyde, *Culture: A Critical Review of Concepts and Definitions*. Cambridge: Peabody Museum, 1952.

Mead, Margaret, and Bunzel, Ruth (eds.), *The Golden Age of Anthropology*. New York: Braziller, 1960.

Michener, James, *Hawaii*. New York: Random House, 1959. (Novel.)

Radin, Paul, *Primitive Man as Philosopher*. New York: Appleton-Century-Crofts, 1927.

Thompson, Laura, *Toward a Science of Mankind*. New York: McGraw-Hill, 1961.

Tylor, Edward B., *Primitive Culture*. 5th ed. London: J. Murray, 1929.

4

CULTURE: PHILOSOPHIC PERSPECTIVES

Metacultural Assumptions of Culture

Like all scientific concepts, culture is undergirded with assumptions or presuppositions. These are not always recognized by scientists of culture, any more than they are recognized by scientists of, say, the geological level of nature. We call the assumptions or presuppositions of culture *meta*cultural because they lie, strictly speaking, beyond or above or beneath an exclusively scientific description. And since philosophy is itself sometimes defined as the critical study of assumptions, let us for present purposes call the philosophy of culture a metacultural discipline.

The introductory section noted that each of the great ideas is to be studied in three major steps—first, an elaboration of the nature of the idea as commonly understood by authorities; second, an attempt to interpret philosophic aspects of the idea; third, consideration especially from our own point of view of the educational significance of the idea in the light of the two preceding steps. Thus, it should be clearly understood that this chapter deals with the second of the three steps. Meanwhile, it is desirable to look for educational implications and thus to anticipate what will be discussed in the following chapter.

The nature of culture was depicted in the preceding chapter in terms of a model having three interrelated dimensions: order, process, and goals. Let us follow a parallel approach to the metacultural level by relating philosophic concepts to each of the three dimensions. In other words, we propose to utilize that branch of philosophy called ontology to clarify the reality of cultural order. Similarly, let us think of cultural process primarily in terms of its epistemological features, and cultural goals primarily in terms of axiology. We emphasize "primarily" because it is unnecessary to contend that the only problems arising when we look critically at cultural order are ontological, that the only problems of cultural process are epistemological or, finally, that the only problems of cultural goals are axiological. Nevertheless, it is our intention to focus on a few of the respective connections between reality, knowledge, and value, on the one hand, and order, process, and goals, on the other hand.

Recall from Chapter 2 that education may be interpreted by means of several great organizing categories of educational philosophy, such as perennialism, essentialism, progressivism, and reconstructionism. Here, we hope to draw upon some of these categories where they help us to see more clearly the theoretical bases of culture. It should always be remembered, however, that these are not to be regarded as "systems" of philosophy, but rather as ways of unifying and interpreting complex experiences.

The Reality of Cultural Order

One of the most interesting contributions to the study of culture is Alfred L. Kroeber's concept of the *superorganic*. Kroeber, widely regarded as the greatest American anthropologist since Franz Boas, contended in a famous essay published in 1917 that culture has a reality of its own which, although entirely natural and subject to scientific explanation, cannot be reduced to "lower" forms of nature. The forms just below the superorganic or cultural might be regarded as the "organic" level of nature— that is, the level of biological phenomena. Culture, however, is a level above that of the merely organic. It has emerged from the organic, to be sure, but, like other emergent levels of nature that have evolved from lower levels, culture has acquired its own distinctive features that are explicable in their own scientific terms.

In the latter years of his life, Kroeber radically modified his original conception of the superorganic as culture. Nevertheless, the theory that culture can be understood best as an organic level of nature above that of other levels remains a fruitful one.

The American anthropologist who has most persistently defended the original superorganic conception is probably Leslie White. Especially in *The Science of Culture*, White argues that because it has an existence of its own, culture also generates itself. Culture causes culture, as it were. Thus, the order of culture is subject to its own laws, just as the order of the biological level of nature is subject to its own laws. The primary anthropological problem becomes, from this viewpoint, chiefly one of discovering the laws inherent in the superorganic character of that reality called culture. These laws are located most centrally in the *patterns* of culture. For example, in every culture, and sometimes across several cultures, we are able to discover patterns of language that can be explained in terms of orderly relationships of symbols. Patterns of custom, such as marriage relationships, are also to be found both quite differently among various cultures and also quite similarly among some cultures. To search for, discover, and formulate the laws of language or the laws of marriage as they exist in culture is not an easy task. Most of it, indeed, remains as yet unaccomplished. Nevertheless, from a superorganic viewpoint, the task of anthropology is to seek and, if possible, to find them so that they can then be formulated in as exact scientific terms as possible.

The metacultural assumption implicit in this viewpoint of cultural order may be associated with a cluster of philosophic beliefs that we shall characterize as belonging to *ontological realism*. By this is meant (in contrast to "classical realism," with which we are not now concerned) that reality is real in the sense that all objects of nature can be perceived directly or indirectly by the senses, that these objects have an existence of their own, and that they are related to one another by equally objective laws of their own. Thus, culture too is an objective reality, just as are other levels of nature. The facts and events of culture are real in the same sense as, let us say, stars, rocks, plants, or animals.

Some ontological realists have been called *historical material-ists* because they hold not only that culture has an objective real-ity which generates itself but that this occurs according to historical laws which are explicable in terms of the utilization of material energy in increasingly complex ways. That is, the spa-tiotemporal order of culture is to be viewed most fundamentally according to ways people channel the energies of nature in order to produce economic goods. This production varies from histor-ical period to historical period: a simple agricultural society is limited to human and perhaps animal energy, whereas an indus-trial society learns to harness the energy latent in coal or water power. The patterns of culture now beginning to arise will be rad-ically different from those of the agricultural or industrial cultures we have thus far known because the forms of nuclear energy now being developed will inevitably transform human life—if, of course, they do not first destroy life.

Ontological realism, whether it is called historical materialism or something else, is an impressive way of interpreting the reality of culture, but it is not the only way. A related but far from iden-tical view of the reality of culture is to be found among those who see the objective patterns of cultural history, not in such materi-alistic terms as energy, but in terms of what is called by philoso-phers *objective idealism*. The concept of idealism is by no means easy for a beginner in philosophy to grasp. For now, however, it is perhaps enough to recall that this theory of reality assumes that, although reality is governed by its own objective laws of stability and change, the "stuff" of reality is not "material" but rather "spiritual" in character. In different terms, the real world is best understood by analyzing the processes of the human psyche and then projecting these into a conception of the processes of the universe.

Is it possible for one to hold a kind of superorganic view of culture and yet to be an idealist in one's metacultural assump-tions? We think that it is. One such proponent is the philosophically minded sociologist Pitirim Sorokin. In his *The Crisis of Our Age*, among other books, Sorokin tries to establish the basic laws of the history of culture which, despite their complexity, follow in a certain sequence, one upon the other, and are primarily characterized by the way human beings think and feel and then behave according to their thinking and feeling. Culture has an objective reality, but this reality is spiritual in its innermost nature.

Now it is perfectly possible, of course, for students to view the nature of culture through the eyes of a White or a Sorokin without ever becoming aware of the presuppositions from which either the objective realist or the objective idealist proceeds in his allegedly scientific treatment of culture. We are afraid, indeed, that such awareness is the exception rather than the rule. Both White and Sorokin speak and write with the prestige of science to support them, although both, in fact, approach culture from metacultural postures that are, to say the least, debatable.

One becomes especially conscious of such metacultural assumptions when one looks at culture from a radically different viewpoint from that of the superorganic as an "objective" (whether material or spiritual) level of reality. Let us call this the *operational* viewpoint. Again, in simplest form, it means negatively that culture, though made up of real facts and events, does not in and of itself have a separate and objective reality at all. Positively, it means that culture is a concept that men have invented by abstracting or drawing from a vast range of human experience. This abstraction is a formulation or intellectual instrument by which we may then more clearly perceive, understand, and perhaps even affect such experience. The word "operational" refers, of course, to the widely influential position in the philosophy of science that regards all basic concepts of science as symbolic shorthand interpretations of particular phases of nature (inanimate and animate alike) which, when utilized as tools of analysis, enable the scientist to give meaning to what he is examining. As he develops this meaning, he thereby clarifies what before had been puzzling. Sometimes, he then moves on to directing and even controlling those phases of nature that before had defied him.

The key, then, is one of meaning: an idea or concept is not a mirror of some objective reality; it is rather a conceptual tool that man has devised to explain reality so that he can make sense of it and even use it to his own advantage.

The operational view of culture is associated with anthropologists such as Bronislaw Malinowski, the later Kroeber, and Clyde Kluckhohn. All these experts, although not in identical ways, interpret culture operationally. They are centrally interested in *how human phenomena function* when examined through the lens of culture, and they hold that the function of any cultural phenomenon is the clue to its meaning. For example, if we are to understand why people in one culture wear different clothing from that worn by people of another culture, it is simple for us to see that the variation in custom is here primarily functional: an African obviously wears much less clothing than an Eskimo because the climates of the two cultures require radically different kinds of protection. In the same way, we are able to operate upon thousands of other cultural patterns and thereby derive a clearer understanding of them.

It is important to reemphasize that the operational view of cultural reality does not deny that the data or phenomena of culture have an objective and real existence. Clothing styles are certainly objects that can be observed; so too can the countlessly more complex manifestations of culture, such as religious ceremonials. In this sense, the objective realist or idealist has a point when he insists upon the external "thereness" of human phenomena. But the crucial matter is the *meaning* of these phenomena—a meaning that emerges as we view them by means of the instruments of cultural interpretation. To understand what a clothing custom means, we must operate upon it by examining its function in the specific kind of human order where it can be observed. So, too, with a religious custom.

Cultural order always involves patterns of human relationship, and the meaning of these patterns is what the anthropologist often is most concerned with. Thus, the order of a family, where descent is patrilineal or matrilineal, for example, becomes meaningful when we study the functions of a given type of kinship or-der. Clearly, such an order did not just develop by accident; there must be reasons for one type of descent in one culture, for another type in a second.

The search for explanations by operating with culture—or more exactly, with the many concepts, such as vertical order, of which culture is the most inclusive—is so far from simple that countless human phenomena remain unexplained. Neverthe-less, that the operational approach to cultural order is quite dif-ferent in its metacultural assumptions from the superorganic may be clarified by comparing the two in the light of educational philosophies.

The superorganic approach to cultural order is congenial to both the essentialist and perennialist orientations, but we shall limit our attention chiefly to the former. Please recall from Chapter 2 that essentialism in its typical formulation is charac-terized by an ontology that is either realistic or idealistic or a combination of both. We do not, of course, deny that realism and idealism are different philosophic conceptions in many ways; we are only saying that essentialism as a philosophy of education rests upon either or both of these ontological conceptions. Seen in cultural perspective, the ontological differences within it prove, indeed, to be more a matter of academic disputation than of very great consequence in terms of the role that essentialist education plays as an enculturative agent. In this perspective, es-sentialism no longer remains a mere intellectual construction to be studied as a self-contained body of thought; rather, it proves to be a consistent and powerful way of reinforcing metacultural assumptions beneath the superorganic view of cultural reality.

To be sure, few essentialists have derived their conception of education directly from anthropologists. On the contrary, some of our conspicuous essentialists (James Bryant Conant, say) do not seem noticeably concerned about the nature of culture as one of the most potent ideas of modern civilization. But this is not the point. We are interested now in the way essentialism serves culture, not in tracing the influences that have given it shape. Our chief conclusion is that, regardless of its sponsors or of variations among them, essentialism provides powerful theoretical support for the common view that education's primary role is to induct each generation into the objective order of culture—an order that has already emerged in nature and is now waiting to be perceived and transmitted according to its own inherent laws. In short, the essentialist, both in his systematic theory and in the enculturative practices that stem from that theory, shares a central metacultural belief. This is the belief that culture is a superorganic self-generating reality which, whether finally interpreted in realist of idealist terms, it is the first business of education to recognize as accurately as possible in order to perpetuate as strictly as possible.

The operational approach to culture, on the other hand, has close affinity to the progressivist and reconstructionist views of education. Confining ourselves again to the former, progressivists hold an operational theory of culture in the respect that they believe its members should learn how to interpret the meaning of various patterns of culture, not so much for the purpose of perpetuating them—although this role is also a necessary one—but, most importantly, for the purpose of modifying them through such operations. Because culture is not an objective order to which human beings are subject and by which they are strictly determined, but rather an abstraction *from* human experience that enables man to develop more effective meaning and control of important levels *of* human experience, the profound although often implicit sense of cultural conservation that the essentialist encourages is not nearly as strong in progressivist theory as it is in essentialism.

Here again, the point is not that progressivist educators consciously derive their approach to education from an operational interpretation of culture as such (although to some degree they may do so); it is rather that the operational idea of culture derives from a philosophy of science that emerges educationally in progressivist thought and practice.

But even this way of putting the relationship is not very helpful. What is important is that, when education is interpreted in terms of its cultural context, the progressivist philosophy of education is the *counterpart* of an operational view of culture. One reinforces the other. Education is thereby conceived as an active *re*-creative agent of enculturation to a far greater degree than in the case of the essentialist-superorganic partnership.

To close our discussion of the ontological problem of cultural order, we emphasize that the superorganic view, as reflected in essentialism, is still in all probability the more dominant of the two educational philosophies that we have considered in this section—more dominant despite its frequent lack of explicit awareness of its own metacultural assumptions. This assertion is supported when we scan the history of education. Limiting our review only to the modern Western world, a large part of its traditional schooling has undoubtedly been essentialist in general character. It has been a kind of schooling that has assumed the objective reality of the universe and of culture as a part of the universe, which it is the business of their inhabitants to become aware of in order that this objective reality can be effectively understood and adjusted to from generation to generation.

Essentialist schools, presupposing as they do either a realist or idealist ontology, or a fusion of both, are therefore allies of ontological realism or idealism in the superorganic sense. Their support of this metacultural orientation has been a loyal one—so loyal that, without much question, the great majority of children in the schools not only of America but of other countries grow into citizens habituated to believe that, in the last analysis, man does not make culture but rather that culture makes man— culture, please remember, conceived as a superorganic reality governed by its own objective and irrevocable regularities.

Knowledge in the Process of Culture

Recall our contention in Chapter 3 that the most fundamental process of culture is that of "acquiring." How do we acquire culture? Clearly, the central answer is: through learning. Here, then, is enough reason for relating that branch of philosophy called "epistemology" to the acquiring process. If we acquire through learning, are we not then involved in knowledge-getting or, still more simply, knowing? And when we are knowing, are we not inescapably engaged in truth-seeking as well? Surely when we claim to know something about, say, an artifact such as a knife we also assume that we know it truly.

This does not mean, please recall, that knowing is necessarily intellectual. Like learning in general, knowing may not take place in a purely conscious way at all. We acquire, we learn, and therefore we know by a great variety of sociopsychological experiences, some of them chiefly intellectual, some of them emotional or visceral, many of them integral with processes of acquiring that include bodily and often group actions of typically overt kinds.

Thus, epistemology, as the philosophic study of the criteria of knowledge, appears in the perspective of culture as a quite different discipline than it does at the hands of formal philosophers. Epistemology is the handmaiden of cultural acquiring, just as ontology, the philosophic study of reality, is the handmaiden of cultural order. At the same time, while culture certainly helps to shape epistemological theory, this does not mean that epistemology has no retroactive effect upon culture. It, in turn, helps us to understand more clearly the process of acquiring culture by means of knowledge-getting. Particularly, we may determine whether some forms of this process generate truth more dependably than other forms. Unless what we acquire is reliable knowledge, we should be learning in ways that in the long run can only lead to the catastrophes of error and falsehood.

But how can we know reliably or truly? This question can be effectively answered only when it is determined how learning takes place in culture. Here, we return to metacultural assumptions. Just a little investigation reveals that the scientists of culture no more proceed from the same metacultural assumptions when they try to resolve issues of learning and knowledge than they do in the case of cultural reality.

We find, for example, that quite a number of anthropologists regard the learning process as chiefly one of *conditioning*. Any student of psychology at once recognizes here the general and loosely bounded position known as *behaviorism*—namely, the position that human beings, like all animals, learn by responding to the stimuli of an outside environment. Behaviorism has developed a variety of technical formulations—the original orthodox theory of the psychologist John Watson no longer being acceptable to most experts. Nevertheless, however many varieties of conditioning theory there may be, the central notion of acquiring through conditioning is common to them all.

Moreover, some recent students have insisted that the introduction of psychoanalytic concepts does not so much alter the basic process of conditioning as to deepen it. *Psychoanalysis* focuses upon another and very important way in which conditioning occurs—that is, through largely unconscious influences induced especially by parents in the first years of life, but also continuously by other members of the culture and subculture to which every human being belongs. Learning, according to this theory, is primarily a process of personality formation by way of emotional responses to the stimuli of those individuals and groups closest to the child.

The connection of learning as conditioning to the superorganic theory of cultural order should at once become apparent. Realists, particularly, tend to support a stimulus-response theory of learning and therefore to presuppose that the individual is exposed to the attitudes and habits of a culture through processes that are reinforced by repetition, by the pleasures of reward and the pains of punishment, and by other reactions which behavioristic psychologists such as Clark Hull and Frederick Skinner have attempted to generalize in the form of laws.

More strictly in terms of epistemology, the metacultural assumption of behaviorists is something like this: truth is the product of man's effective grasp of the basic rules, skills, customs, and knowledge already embodied in the given objective reality, including the reality of culture. Educationally, the acquiring process is chiefly one of adjustment. As Merle Curti has demonstrated in his brilliant examination of E. L. Thorndike, who was probably the most influential educational psychologist in American history, the behaviorist is an ally, if often unwittingly, of the kind of educator who believes that the school is primarily an agency of cultural reinforcement.

Again, however, it is possible to show how quite different assumptions from these may be operating in other cultural interpretations of the acquiring process. Parallel, for example, to the operational approach to cultural reality, acquiring can be regarded as much more of a creative process than the behaviorist leads us to assume. According to this second view, man *acquires* by a process of *inquiring* into the nature of his culture. And inquiring, as John Dewey (easily the most influential philosopher of progressivism) implies in such a book as *Freedom and Culture*, is man's capacity to engage actively and critically in the events of his cultural experience—to take them apart, as it were, and to rearrange them in more satisfying, efficient, workable ways than before.

Even the mind of the human being is conceived differently from the way it is by the realist-behaviorist school. Whereas the latter tends to think of mind as a kind of material or mechanical substance capable of absorbing the knowledge of the outside world, including the outside culture, the second viewpoint (which we may call *functionalism*) thinks of mind more as a verb than as a noun—that is, as a special way of acting called "inquiring" or "intelligent functioning." According to this view, the process requires continuous modification of the *habits* of acquiring. Man learns thereby to modify such habits by awareness of the obstacles that stand in the way of his onward course, by analyzing these obstacles as carefully as possible, and by trying out new ways of overcoming them when old ways prove to be unworkable. In Dewey's terms, human beings carry on *transactions* with their environment, and thus with their culture, through which both "parties" to the transaction are altered.

This second view of the knowing process does not deny that minds are immersed in and thus conditioned by cultural patterns. But minds, it contends, draw from cultural experience in order to develop more effective means of returning to that experience. One might go so far as to say that inquiring, from this viewpoint, is a feedback process developed in conjunction with, but also in addition to, the acquiring process defined primarily in terms of conditioning. That is, the inquiring mind feeds back its inquiries to the culture from which it derives them and thereby alters some feature of the culture from what it was before.

The chief philosophies of education that come to mind when we look at the acquiring process in these alternative ways are, once more, the essentialist and progressivist. The essentialist tends to take a conditioning view of learning, as may be exemplified in the work of an American realistic essentialist, Ross Finney—one of the few of that orientation with a strong background in the social sciences, including anthropology. In *A Sociological Philosophy of Education*, a great deal of stress is quite consistently placed upon what Finney calls "passive mentation"—a process of acquiring the social heritage (superorganically interpreted) by placing the learner in a position of receptivity to the skills, laws, and contents already determined by the objective culture.

By contrast, the progressivist assumes that when men acquire knowledge of culture they do not and certainly need not engage merely in "passive mentation" but may learn also how to inquire into the conditions that have compelled them to acquire that knowledge in habitual ways. Such inquiring, in other words, often reveals that what has become known through routine processes of acquiring proves to be much less reliable and, hence, less productive of truth than tradition or custom had blandly assumed. The positive side of this awareness is a fresh incentive to search for more reliable and more productive ways of acquiring knowledge—an awareness which, although probably very gradually developed over centuries (it has not developed very far even yet in concrete educational practice) leads to an active reconstructive conception of learning defined as a transaction in which both poles of the epistemological equation—the knower and the known, the learner and the culture learned—are both modified.

The contrasting implications of the essentialist and the progressivist interpretations of the acquiring process for everyday schools are, then, very far-reaching. We propose to look at a few of these implications in the pages ahead. At this stage we only wish to reiterate that epistemology is, in a sense, at the root of the process of culture, but that this epistemology is not of only one kind. Actually, there are other kinds than the two we have chosen to emphasize—for example, those characteristic of Eastern cultures, as F. S. C. Northrop has tried to show in *The Meeting of East and West*. At the same time, it is important to emphasize our disagreement with Northrop in his own contention that it is epistemology (and other dimensions of philosophy) that somehow shape the various patterns of culture. A more nearly correct view is that it is the patterns of culture that shape the nature of various philosophies. But the latter do undoubtedly contribute to the effort of every culture to make itself meaningful to its constituents, and in performing this service epistemology comes to play an important part in the articulation and implementation of the cultural process itself.

Goal-Seeking in Culture

We turn now to the third "angle" of our "triangular" model—cultural goals. If it is true, as earlier contended, that all cultures have implicit or explicit goals—that is, purposes toward which they endeavor to move with some sense of direction—then it is also true that all cultures have more or less articulate sets of values that symbolize rightness or wrongness, goodness or badness, beauty or ugliness. But the nature of cultural goals, like that of order and process, may be interpreted again in conflicting ways, depending upon the metacultural assumptions from which it is approached.

Let us consider, as one such approach, the view that the values of culture are primarily determined by the basic interest of human beings—by their striving for satisfaction of needs and wants. Here is the view of anthropologists such as Malinowski, who, in his *Freedom and Civilization*, takes the view that we must understand the goals of people in terms of their aim to satisfy desires. These range all the way from the physiological hungers of food and sex to the more subtle but nevertheless equally genuine sociopsychological wants of recognition and cooperation.

Such an approach to cultural goals may be expressed axiologically as a *functional theory of ethics*—ethics being defined here as the philosophic study of moral conduct. Also, it inclines toward the expectation that the interests of human beings everywhere in the world can be found to have many common denominators, no matter how diversified cultures might otherwise be. Thus, one of the typical contentions of this approach is that we need to study the values of people *cross-culturally*—that is, to compare one culture with another to see how far their goals function in both similar and different ways. This kind of study leads some anthropologists (Kluckhohn is one) to believe that the venerable issue discussed in the last chapter—namely, whether goals are relative or universal—is resolved by holding that actually they are of both kinds. For us to assume that cultural values are limited to each individual culture is just as invalid as to assume that the values of all cultures are identical.

Another approach to the problem of goals that has a long philosophic history is the theory that cultures are moving progressively toward an ultimate end that is somehow inherent in the order and process of culture. According to this theory, goals are the driving force of all cultural change in that they provide the "magnets" that draw men onward and, in a sense, upward toward perfection. This view is no longer widely maintained by scientists of culture, although it was vaguely assumed in some of the earlier ones—perhaps even Tylor—insofar as they believed that cultures evolved from "savagery" to "civilization" in a kind of inevitable sequence. Also, a case could be offered to demonstrate that students of culture who proceed from certain perennialist beliefs (Father Teilhard de Chardin is one) are of this persuasion.

In ontological terms, the view that culture—indeed, the whole universe—is moving inevitably toward an ultimate goal is called *teleology*. The nature of the goal may vary according to different theorists, however. Marxists, for example, hold that it is the "classless society"—the Communist ideal of pure economic freedom through public ownership and control of all means of production. Those of Father Teilhard's faith conceive that the ultimate goal is eternal salvation, and that all cultural processes are in one way or another a means to this perfect and final end.

Returning once more to the categories of educational philosophy, one may hold that the first view of the goal problem—exemplified by Malinowski—is perhaps closer to what we have called the reconstructionist orientation than to the others. Reconstructionists hold that the delineation of human goals is to be achieved through cross-cultural research that enlists not only anthropology but all the sciences of human behavior, such as psychiatry and political science. They insist that if only a fraction as much money and energy were spent in the study of human experience, including individual and social desires, as is spent in, say, the field of space rocketry, it would be possible to move at a much faster pace toward understanding the universal values of culture.

The reconstructionist educator also takes the position that not only is it possible to *describe* the desires of human beings by such research, but that it is possible to arrive at much greater consensus than we have thus far achieved as to the *desirability* of the most important cross-cultural goals. In other words, description could lead to both *prescription* and *proscription* of goals—both to those that are recommended as culturally desirable and to those that are condemned as culturally undesirable. This position compels us to consider a comparatively novel way of validating values—that is, of demonstrating not only that some values are in fact the goals of culture but that they deserve to be striven for because they are eminently worthwhile.

The bridging of the gap between described values, on the one hand, and prescribed—that is, *normative*—values, on the other hand, is suggested by the reconstructionist theory of "social consensus." At this moment, we limit our explanation to the simple steps that consensus embraces. It is necessary first to consider the maximum *evidence* available as to whether certain goals—sexual satisfaction is one—are in fact accepted by all or most cultures. (This example, of course, at once proves that such acceptance can be virtually universal, although even so common a goal is not 100 percent universal, since celibacy is preferred by a few individuals). The second step requires *communication* both among members of one culture and also among cultures that the evidence is what it claims to be. The third step is the endeavor to express as wide *agreement* as possible upon the basis of the evidence communicated. The fourth step is to act in order to test out the agreement by *observation and experience*—thereby determining whether verbalized testimony harmonizes with behavioral testimony. (The example of sexual satisfaction has the support of uncounted numbers of research studies, historical documents, and esthetic creations from poetry to painting.)

Referring back for a moment to the knowledge-getting process, one might say that social consensus involves both inquiring and acquiring. That is, it involves the kind of social inquiring necessary in collecting and comparing evidence and in reaching maximum communication about that evidence. It involves social acquiring in the sense that the aim of the collecting and communicating of evidence is to achieve as much active agreement as possible about desirable goals on the basis of the evidence and the communication. The major process of culture, acquiring, is thereby linked with cultural goals and the seeking of them—a good indication of why it is impossible in the experience of living cultures to separate any one of the three dimensions (order, process, or goals) from the other two. It indicates, also, why reconstructionist education, though concerned with achieving desirable goals by practice with social consensus at every possible stage of enculturation, recognizes that cultural goals in turn demand both effective processes of achieving them and effective orders of human relationship within which these processes may function.

By contrast, the perennialist theory of cultural goals does not assume that one achieves them primarily by a social or public process of acquiring and inquiring, but rather that the goals of man, already inherent as they are in the nature of culture and universe, will be attained if you and I can somehow learn to recognize the absolute laws of reality, knowledge, and value necessary to their attainment and can then abide by these laws to the utmost. In this recognition of objective law, the perennialist reminds one of the essentialist's attitude toward superorganic order, but he differs from the latter in his insistence that the value-seeking and value-achieving process requires, no less than knowledge-getting, a strong ingredient of *intuition* and even of *revelation*. The ultimate goals of culture are not delineated by a cooperative process of gathering, communicating, and agreeing upon relevant evidence; they are discerned, finally, by one's inherent capacity to discover their character through one's own rational and spiritual power—reinforced, of course, by divine power. Education's most important responsibility is to share in and enhance this discovery.

The distinction between the reconstructionist's and perennialist's approaches to goal-seeking is highlighted by the meaning of *prediction*. The former may to some degree predict the goals of culture—or at least particular, short-range goals—by analysis of the evidence available as to human interests and capacities. Then, utilizing rules of statistical probability, he may anticipate certain outcomes before they actually occur. For example, the goal of adequate shelter for the people of an underdeveloped country such as Puerto Rico has been carefully formulated by its housing agencies. These agencies already know what kind of desire most Puerto Ricans have in this respect, and they agree with the majority of people that this desire is also a worthwhile goal. By carefully formulated plans extending over, say, twenty years, they are able to predict how this goal will probably be achieved.

Perennialists would not necessarily object to this kind of limited prediction, but they would regard it as of such minor consequence that, in their historic cultural activities, they have usually subordinated if not ignored it. For them, the really important predictions of life are not scientifically ascertainable at all but metaculturally guaranteed. Thus, they predict the highest of all goals—salvation—because it is predetermined by the perennial everlasting character of teleological reality itself. There is, for them, no mere probability about it. The ultimate goal of life is the eternity of the spiritual universe, and this is absolutely certain.

Recapitulation

Approaching the nature of culture by way of metacultural assumptions reveals that it may be understood according to different philosophic conceptions of what culture appears to be when pictured in their image. These conceptions, as distinguished from the kind of tri-dimensional scientific model presented in the preceding chapter, are grounded in ontological, epistemological, and axiological beliefs that are often taken so much for granted as to lie beyond or beneath the cultural scientist's usual range of perception or concern.

Thus culture as a reality may be interpreted from the point of view of realistic and/or idealistic essentialism but also from the point of view of an operational theory of culture akin to the progressivist orientation toward education. The first regards education as a superorganic reality, the second, as an abstraction to enable meaningful explanation of complex levels of patterned group behavior.

A similar contrast can be seen in the essentialist and progressivist ways of acquiring culture—ways that reflect different conceptions of epistemology as knowledge-getting. Realist essentialists emphasize behaviorist conditioning; the progressivists, critical inquiring and controlling. Note the term "emphasize," however: often the one theory borrows something from the other.

The problem of goals in culture is to some extent clarified when the reconstructionist approach is compared with that of the perennialist. The latter regards cultural goals as indigenous with his teleological ontology—thus, presumably assuring their ultimate achievement. The former views them as cross-cultural values that cannot only be described scientifically but prescribed by the fullest possible operation of social consensus in its several steps. Here, again, it is important to note that, for purposes of concise contrast, differences between these philosophies are stressed more than their points of agreement.

It has not been our intention to accomplish more in this chapter than to exemplify ways in which culture can be interpreted in terms of several kinds of metacultural assumptions. We find that when the order of culture is viewed through the prism of one ontology, the image of culture is by no means always the same as when it is looked at through another prism. Similarly, varying images appear when we view the process of culture or the goals of culture.

This does not mean that the various and sometimes conflicting philosophic prisms are sufficient explanations of the order, process, and goals of culture; it is truer to say that, culturally, the prisms themselves are the product of different patterns of human life. The superorganic interpretation, for example, cannot be derived simply from either a realist or idealist ontology. Rather, historic periods of culture have themselves been conducive to the development of realist and idealist prisms. The superorganic-essentialist conception of culture gradually emerges from much deeper metacultural attitudes than those of philosophy in any formal sense. It is an expression of one of the most ancient of all human beliefs and practices—namely, that because human beings are, after all, the products of culture, they must learn to accept it in order to play their rightful role as loyal members of it. The operational-progressivist view is much younger in history—the product of a period when people were learning how to take more of a critical, self-conscious, participative part in the fashioning of their cultures.

At the same time, both these views, although the products of cultural experience, have played, in turn, a vital role in shaping culture by providing it with a rationale for what it has all along been struggling to do. While to attribute the cause of cultures to any ontology, epistemology, or axiology is fallacious, equally so is the contention that they have no marked influence upon the cultures that have nourished and sustained them. This reciprocity between philosophy and culture may be understood perhaps most clearly upon the great testing ground of cultural practice—education itself.

Recommended Readings for Chapter 4

Boas, Franz, *Race, Language and Culture*. New York: Macmillan, 1940.

Brameld, Theodore, *Philosophies of Education in Cultural Perspective*. New York: Holt, Rinehart & Winston, 1955. (Interpretations of progressivism, essentialism, and perennialism.)

Conant, James Bryant, *The American High School Today*. New York: McGraw-Hill, 1959.

Curti, Merle, *The Social Ideas of American Educators*. New York: Scribner's, 1935.

Dewey, John, *Freedom and Culture*. New York: Putnam's, 1939; *Knowing and the Known* (with Arthur F. Bentley). Boston: Beacon, 1949; *Reconstruction in Philosophy*. New York: Holt, Rinehart & Winston, 1920.

Finney, Ross L., *A Sociological Philosophy of Education*. New York: Macmillan, 1928.

Hull, Clark L., *A Behavior System*. New Haven: Yale University Press, 1952.

Kroeber, Alfred L., "The Superorganic," reprinted in *The Nature of Culture*. Chicago: University of Chicago Press, 1952.

Malinowski, Bronislaw, *A Scientific Theory of Culture and Other Essays*. Chapel Hill: University of North Carolina Press, 1944; *Freedom and Civilization*. New York: Roy, 1944.

Northrop, F. S. C., *The Meeting of East and West*. New York: Macmillan, 1947.

Skinner, B. F., *Science and Human Behavior*. New York: Macmillan, 1953.

Sorokin, Pitirim, *The Crisis of Our Age*. New York: Dutton, 1941.

Teilhard de Chardin, P., *The Phenomenon of Man*. New York: Harper & Row, 1959.

Watson, John B. *Behaviorism*. New York: Norton, 1930.

White, Leslie. *The Science of Culture*. New York: Farrar, Straus, 1949.

5

THE SCHOOL AS AGENT
OF CULTURE

"Internalizing" the Idea of Culture

We have gone sufficiently far in our exploration of the idea of culture to appreciate that it is much more vast and complex than appeared at first glance. This discovery, of course, will apply to both of the remaining ideas. We move now to the third stage of our study of culture, where we wish to ask what its meaning may be for the practical work of the teacher or other professional educator.

As we do so, it may be helpful here to introduce an added opportunity to learn. One obligation of the serious student is to try in every way he can to *internalize* the great idea with which he is making initial acquaintance. To internalize is to fuse the chief characteristics of that idea with one's own attitudes, feelings, and daily activities. Culture becomes important to us as persons and as teachers only to the extent that such fusion takes place. The often abstract and involved aspects of such a gigantic concept as culture may at first seen so external, so intellectually erudite, that an initiate may quite understandably find trouble in integrating it with his own experience. Yet the real test of whether the effort to understand such an idea has been worthwhile is precisely the degree to which such fusion takes place—or perhaps we would better say, *transfusion*. To internalize is to move from a merely intellectual formulation, on the one hand, to one's own personality (one's own patterns of behavior), on the other hand. When and if we succeed in doing so, we thenceforth actually look at our world differently than we did before. And sometimes in quite unconscious ways, sometimes very deliberately, we then act differently in carrying out our personal and professional tasks. Our bridge-building model tried earlier, in different symbols, to express much the same contention.

The idea of culture, in short—no less and no more than that of class or evolution—is anything but an intellectual patent medicine. One cannot swallow it with the expectation that one is going to be changed in some miraculous, more or less automatic, fashion. There is no possible way in which the author of this book, for example, can compel any reader to internalize a single one of the ideas that are its theme. He is, nevertheless, convinced that any student who approaches, say, the idea of culture seriously and responsibly will in the course of time become a very different kind of person and teacher than he would otherwise be. In some cases such integrating effect will occur months, even years, later. But whenever it does, the school too will begin to undergo transformation. Every school is, in a genuine sense, the creation of those who operate it. Thus, the kinds of learning and control that occur are, from one point of view, the fruits of whatever orientation toward life and education has developed among the members of a culture directly responsible for the enculturative process. Teachers, surely, are among the most important of these members.

Now we are ready to move ahead. What difference does an idea such as culture make to our conception of the school curriculum? What difference does it make to the teaching-learning process? Finally, what difference does it make to the control of education? These issues, we recall, were introduced in the first section as ways to approach the level of educational practice through each one of our central ideas. Here, again, we propose to draw into our discussion the three familiar concepts of order, process, and goals. The curriculum is thus considered in relation to cultural order, teaching-learning in terms of cultural process, and the control of education in view of cultural goals. Familiarity with the preceding two chapters is therefore presupposed.

Problems of the Curriculum:
The Significance of Cultural Order

The concept of cultural order, we remember, enables us to view the total environment fashioned by man in terms of spatio-temporal relations—a shorthand term for the fact that every culture may be viewed both in horizontal and vertical perspective, while yet embracing the past, the present, and the future. This model of cultural order, when it becomes filled with the rich content that such a science as anthropology provides, may now be conceived as a way to organize the curriculum itself.

Many different attempts have recently been made to create a more adequate design for the subject matter that should enter into the curriculum of each major level—elementary, secondary, higher. Innumerable proposals to attain a more effective "general education" on the high school and college levels, for example, have been argued pro and con; some have even been tried out. Yet it is only too apparent that educators still have a great deal of trouble achieving any kind of wide agreement as to what the best conception for unifying the great array of subject matter should be. Some borrow their models from the natural sciences. Others (perennialists, especially) seem to think that general education is best achieved through the great books of all time. We suggest that a neglected, yet fruitful opportunity, lies right before us in the concept of cultural order.

What could this concept contribute to a distinctive way of unifying and integrating the curriculum of general education? One answer lies in a controversial contention—namely, that the central obligation of education for most young people should be basically similar, and that the justification for such similarity lies in the struggles and objectives of human beings themselves. This kind of education should be concerned first of all with the attempt to provide an understanding by the young learner not only of himself but of his relations to others: other groups, other nations, and equally of theirs to him. In short, the study of every subject matter, such as art or science, and the development of every skill, such as language or mathematics, ultimately becomes sanctioned in the degree that each subject matter and each skill contribute both directly and indirectly to the maximum fulfillment of the human personality and of the culture with which it is reciprocal.

The key term "fulfillment" requires, of course, more elaborate explanation than we are able to provide here. A number of social psychologists (Gordon Allport and Abraham Maslow among them) prefer some such term as "self-actualization." By this they mean optimum expression of the whole personality—emotional, intellectual, and physical. The difficulty with this view, however, is that it usually limits itself too narrowly to the individual. The culture concept widens the meaning to include cultural, social, and political actualization. A family, school, or even a nation, is also capable of moving toward greater actualization of its own characteristic powers, although always in reciprocal relation with its individual members. Fulfillment is *both* cultural and personal when it is understood as a standard or norm through which to build good education. The underlying principle may be better understood by the term "complementarity": each of the two concepts depends upon and strengthens the meaning of the others.

Culture, at any rate, points the way to the rebuilding of general education. For culture provides, or could provide, unifying significance for the whole of human experience. Think, for example, what this could mean if we look at the curriculum in terms of the spatial order of culture viewed as widening concentric circles of human relationship. Recall from Chapter 3 that the central core focuses upon problems of intrapersonal and interpersonal relations; that the next wider circle embraces intragroup and intergroup relations (racial, class, and others); and that the widest circle encompasses the relations of whole peoples, nations, and religions. Thus, through this conception of order, we are able to see the world as a vast intricate network of human relations, from the most intimate to that most inclusive of "complex wholes," mankind itself. Thus, too, the study of all the human sciences, from psychiatry to anthropology, becomes integrated and unified. Likewise, the physical sciences could acquire a significance that they never will acquire as long as they are treated as self-contained bodies of subject matter divorced from the great issues of cultural experience.

But, as also has been earlier pointed out, the merely spatial model of culture is defective as long as it lacks the temporal dimension. We need to think of the curriculum of general education not only in terms of the present relationships of people, but in terms both of their roots in the past and their directions toward the future. The latter anticipates the problem of cultural goals, to which we return, but the former suggests the need for intensive study of *history*—history, however, hardly exemplified by the commonly sterile and unmotivated sequences of facts and events characteristic of traditional courses in the field. Actually, there is no good reason why history cannot become an immensely vital part of the curriculum, particularly if reorganized with the resources of such potent philosophers of cultural history as Oswald Spengler and Arnold Toynbee. Usually disregarded except by graduate courses that most students never take, these and like historians could be drawn into the course of study in ways that are pioneering and thrilling to earnest young learners. However debatable their respective interpretations, they provide history with meaningful unity and immense relevance for our fascinating age.

Here it is necessary to introduce a new concept of interpretation. We can better understand the significance of the study of history in a culture-oriented curriculum if we distinguish more clearly between the essentialist approach discussed in the preceding chapter, and the progressivist, also discussed. It will be remembered that the essentialist, directly or indirectly reflecting as he does the superorganic view of culture, tends metaculturally to regard the order of culture as something "out there," already determined and structured beyond the control of individual human beings. We now wish to become much more critical of this viewpoint by asking whether the essentialist (and, incidentally, the perennialist also) is justified in objectifying culture as he does. Thus, the question arises whether he does not transfer an idea from its origin and locus in human thinking to an external status of its own, claiming an independent existence of its own. Many philosophers have called attention to such transference, which they usually call *hypostatization* or *reification*, pointing out that its origin lies deep in primitive habits of thinking—habits characterized by the objectifying of symbols (written, spoken, musical, pictorial) into things with their own power and reality.

But such primitive habits are so characteristically resistant to criticism or modification that they may become engraved in cultural evolution even up to the stage of very sophisticated systems of symbols. Indeed, one finds many of the greatest philosophers, such as Plato and Hegel, projecting concepts of their invention into objective realities—Plato's Idea of Good probably being the most famous instance. In the Middle Ages, this practice developed into prolonged conflict between thinkers who defended it (these defenders are sometimes called *classical realists*) and thinkers who insisted that the objectification of concepts are simple names and not things at all (the historical name for them is *nominalists*). In contemporary philosophy, such great thinkers as Alfred North Whitehead have repeatedly attacked the habit of hypostatization, but others have continued to insist upon the external, indeed eternal, existence of, say, the orderly laws of nature and of man that symbols allegedly express.

Returning now to the study of history in the school, progressivists aware of the metacultural issue are likely to assert that essentialist history is often hypostatized history as well. Because, moreover, the past is regarded as something that is irrevocably finished, it follows that the kind of history provided by the conventional curriculum is intended primarily to develop in young people an attitude of acceptance toward the out-thereness and completeness of historical events. Culturally, such an attitude is likely to encourage a conservative frame of mind toward the social heritage. Hence it is no accident that the essentialist school is usually regarded as an enculturative agent of reinforcement of patterns of culture that have come down to us in the course of time.

The significance of hypostatic approaches to history may be better understood if we contrast them as sharply as possible with the way progressivists would treat the temporal dimension of culture. Here we need to utilize an operational interpretation; that is, as suggested earlier, the contention that culture is actually an intellectual instrument. It explains, and at times rebuilds, those levels of experience that are characterized by the order, process, and goals of human life viewed in its patterned relationships. History, understood now as the temporal phase of cultural order, may also be interpreted as an operational discipline—that is, the past is approached not as a forever-finished record of objective events but as a boundlessly fertile opportunity to interpret and reinterpret the course of human evolution.

Such an approach, although it may seem very strange at first to essentialist-conditioned students, has been developed by a number of recent scholars. We mention only Herbert Muller's *The Uses of the Past*, Richard Heilbroner's *The Future as History*, and Erich Kahler's *Man the Measure*. All these books, in somewhat different ways and not always in strictly operational terms, argue that man continually reshapes the nature of his own history as he draws upon it for light in coping with problems of the present and expectations for the future. This is not intended to mean that the events of history are not objectively real; it does mean that their reality is subject to constant operational reinterpretation and ever fresh utilization. Thereby, the reality of history itself undergoes change.

How, then, would a progressivist include history in general education? If he is consistently operational, he will not, first of all, segregate history from other dimensions of learning experience anywhere nearly as much as do essentialists. Rather, he will regard it as a vast, fruitful resource to be drawn upon in attacking every conceivable kind of problem—including problems only indirectly related to human experience, such as those of the physical sciences. Accordingly, history teachers, in the kind of integrated curriculum suggested by cultural order, become resource persons who constantly and cooperatively work with other teachers.

Of course, a place for separate, concentrated study of historical periods is legitimate also. Such study should be available primarily through elective courses for students who develop special interest in, say, the history of ancient Rome or of modern China. The common core of history required of all students, however, is considered not so much as a separate discipline as it is a reservoir of ever-growing knowledge. The progressivist is insistent that more solid history will be learned in this way by the average student than by any number of standard courses provided by typical high schools and colleges today.

To conclude our discussion of cultural order as a unifying principle for the curriculum of general education, please remember that we have been limited to but a few examples. The practical question, meanwhile, is whether even an inexperienced teacher can involve himself in such an audacious undertaking. We suggest that he can—that even in a traditional school he will view his specialization with quite a different attitude if he is governed by the culture concept than if he is not. Nor do we limit ourselves to the teacher of history. Rather, teachers in any field can, in some degree, permeate their subject matter with aspects of cultural order by the way they emphasize and the way they select issues and materials for careful attention.

More than this, the conscientious teacher, once he becomes convinced of the importance of cultural order, can join with other teachers in rethinking the curriculum. In this effort, he must also, of course, enlist the interest of students, parents, and administrators. But when we remember what was suggested at the beginning of this chapter—that one important reason good schools develop at all is because good teachers want them to develop—then his sense of dedication to the task of rebuilding is prerequisite to every step of accomplishment.

Teaching-Learning and the Cultural Process

We return now to the second major dimension of culture—process—looking at it this time with concern for sample problems of teaching and learning. Clearly, we have not ignored them thus far: the essentialist and progressivist postures toward history, for example, already indicate two ways by which the teacher functions and, simultaneously, two ways by which the learner functions in relation to the teacher.

Again, a moment of recapitulation. The preceding chapter tried to show that the key to cultural process lies in Tylor's term "acquiring"—but that metaculturally the term appears to suggest different things to different interpreters. Thus the realist essentialist way of acquiring is primarily by means of conditioning, while the progressivist way of *ac*quiring is primarily through *in*quiring. In different words, the essentialist presupposes a psychology of learning epitomized in some such term as "passive mentation," while the progressivist takes a more functional and organismic approach through which acquiring as learning involves active and critical transactions with the cultural and physical environment.

In discussing the curriculum above, we indicated our sympathy with progressivist approaches to curriculum remaking. We express the same kind of preference here. The point made several times, however, to the effect that philosophies of education are not to be regarded as separate objective systems but rather as on a continuum of overlapping operational meanings, can now be underscored. We wish here to give full credit to an important emphasis in the essentialist theory of teaching-learning that, in the light of our sharp critique above, could easily be overlooked. This contribution stems from the recognition of Leslie White and other realist-oriented anthropologists that cultural patterns are exceedingly "tough"—that is, powerful not only in their control over the habits and attitudes of people but in their resistance to deliberate modification. Any kind of effective education needs, consequently, to assess with maximum clarity and honesty the stubborn obstacles that stand in the way of effecting any kind of planned change in patterns of cultural order. Essentialists in education are, from this point of view, again the ally of superorganic anthropologists: both perform a useful role in calling persistent attention to the hurdles that must be leaped if any kind of organized human action aimed at modifying the customs, habits, mores, and other attributes of the inherited culture can ever hope to succeed.

The point is now underscored by introducing another fruitful concept: that of *modal personality*—a concept developed a few years ago especially by the anthropologist Ralph Linton working with psychiatrists such as Abram Kardiner. What modal personality means is that in every particular culture a kind of personality gestalt or pattern exists—discoverable if one searches hard enough—which mirrors in various ways the dominant patterns of that culture. Modal personality is never, of course, identical with any living individual; after all, it is an abstraction, a mode, of many individuals. In this sense it is also operational. Yet we may also find that personalities do converge toward patterned characteristics of emotion, thought, and practice—these characteristics deriving primarily from the kind of culture in which a given group of personalities grow up. (Characteristics that are genetic, such as skin color, or unique to an individual, such as voice tone, are not therefore included in the meaning of the term.) The arduous research necessary to delineate the modal personality of any culture demands close cooperation between anthropologists and psychiatrists or other scientists of man. For this reason, the new rapprochement between these two groups of experts is sometimes said to center in the "culture-and-personality movement."

It would be possible to illustrate what is meant by modal personality through a hypothetical example: an urban street gang of adolescents, whose members have developed ways of distinguishing themselves from others in their communities. Members consider themselves a family and take on particular ways of walking, greeting each other, signaling with secret hand signs, and wearing clothes that identify them as members. They are suspicious of strangers, highly sensitive to perceived acts of disrespect, and feel an obligation to respond to disrespect toward the group with violence. In addition, the members have their own personalities. Nevertheless, when together, they act in ways that are characteristic of the gang's modal personality.

Such a work as that of John W. M. Whiting and Irvin C. Child, *Child Training and Personality*, also demonstrates convincingly the potent influence that the subculture of the family exerts upon the shaping of modal personality. For example, a culture in which the typical attitude of the father and mother toward the child is rigidly authoritarian is bound to shape the child's lifelong character (in an injurious fashion, incidentally), even though the child leaves the parents at a very early age for another kind of environment. Here, conditioning as a process of learning is obviously primary, but Whiting and Child, in common with a number of other students of culture and personality, emphasize the conditioning that occurs in the shaping of emotional patterns by influences that are often quite unconscious—a reflection of the psychiatric orientation of many recent researchers in this field.

What practical value may the teacher draw from these remarks? Perhaps the most apparent and yet important one is this: the young personalities gathered together in the average classroom become much more maturely understood in the degree that the teacher is qualified to look for and delineate the kind of modal personality that is to be expected in the respective culture and subculture where they happen to live. By the same token, the teacher cannot possibly give top-level professional guidance to the learner until he is as familiar as possible with the cultural patterns that have permeated so deeply the personality of every child.

In terms of professional preparation, this also means that no teacher is qualified whose only exposure to the sciences of human behavior has been through conventional courses in psychology. Typically, these courses, although they often pay brief attention to cultural influences, are negligent in their regard for the impact of the cultural process as it presses relentlessly upon personality structure from the very day of the child's birth—indeed, in the prenatal period as well. Many of the perplexities and frustrations from which teachers suffer in their relations to children's personalities could be sharply reduced if teachers had the opportunity to spend part of their professional time examining and interpreting, especially with anthropological guidance, the conditioning forces that work invisibly but relentlessly beyond the windows of their classrooms.

The potential contributions of an essentialist-superorganic approach to the process of acquiring (those just suggested are rarely as yet actual) must not, however, allow us to generalize too far in their favor. The trouble with this kind of learning is that it often commits the error of assuming that because it is partly right, therefore it must be altogether right. To say, for example, that the modal personality of every learner is heavily conditioned by the acquiring of family or community order does not justify the inference that the teacher's first responsibility is to help children adjust to such an order.

The metacultural assumptions of the progressivist are therefore needed to counterbalance the one-sidedness of an essentialist-oriented interpretation. According to progressivism, the teacher's role, as already noted, is one of recognizing as sensitively as possible the influences of culture upon learners while at the same time encouraging them to the utmost to develop skills and habits of creative modification. In this approach, progressivism can also find (although it has too seldom looked for) support from the science of culture itself.

Take one example. Anyone who has studied primitive cultures knows that one of their most universal rituals centers in the phenomenon of puberty. When a boy or girl reaches an age in the neighborhood of thirteen, the culture arranges to induct him or her into adult institutions and practices—a time often of great solemnity and prolonged ceremony. Carryovers are to be found in many so-called civilized cultures, such as the Jewish rite of Bar Mitzvah, which can be observed in hundreds of American communities.

Now, the import of this phenomenon for our interest is not only that it enables the novitiate to learn in dramatic and poignant ways what the culture considers to be of grave important to its *ethos*—its way of life—but in addition it performs the function of impressing upon the young in unforgettable fashion that they are on the threshold of mature responsibility, that they are no longer merely carefree children but the heirs of their own ethos. Puberty rites thus have the added importance of inducting the young warrior, say, into the new and solemn stage of his life when he begins to share in fighting, defending, hunting, and other tasks indispensable to the preservation and continuation of his culture. Nor are tasks such as these, if one examines them carefully, merely the products of conditioning. To acquire facility as a hunter or fishermen involves skills which, in turn, demand complex inquiring abilities—often imaginative and resourceful abilities of searching, trapping, and hunting the wild game upon which his tribe depends for sustenance.

No tribal young man or woman, therefore, crosses from childhood to adolescence and maturity without realizing that he or she is about to take an active responsible role in the life of his or her own people. This active role frequently tests not only his bravery but his competence to meet unexpected crises with such qualities as audacity, foresight, and cooperation. It is hardly too much to say, indeed, that most of the important advances in either so-called primitive or so-called civilized cultures have stemmed from the ability with which their adult members succeeded in learning how to carry on and to redirect the processes of culture. These processes demand, in the full sense of that term, continuous inquiry.

To punctuate the contention, let us for a moment imagine how pottery may have been developed in the primitive world. Here is a thirsty savage, wandering along the edge of a stream. He happens to note a piece of stone with a concave surface that has caught and held water after a storm. Instead of kneeling down to lap up water from the stream, as had been his habit, he lifts up the stone and drinks. Then remembering his mate and baby in a nearby cave, he fills the stone again and carries it to them.

This kind of simple incident could easily have led to the chipping of stone surfaces into concave shapes in order to serve as storage vessels. It could have led, too, to the drying of mud into more varied shapes to hold and preserve water, grain, fruits, meats, and other foods. Here, the inquiring process is once more in full operation. The simple function of conserving water has evolved, over many scores of centuries, to the highly complex processes that we know today—a few of them, such as refrigeration by electricity, almost as young as we ourselves.

The important inference is, then, that the *inquiring dimension of acquiring* is as universal to the cultural process as conditioning itself. As anthropologist H. G. Barnett demonstrates in his work *Innovation,* cultures constantly, both in small or large ways, modify their established routines and institutions in order to function more competently and successfully than they did before.

Returning again to practical problems of modern learning and teaching, we now see that cultural theory and research afford solid ground upon which to approach these problems with an innovating attitude. Indeed, the contention of some essentialist educators that the school has no legitimate role as an agent of cultural change fails to stand up in the face of such research. The attitude of innovation, when consciously and deliberately developed by the teacher within a cultural matrix, not only negates this contention, but it influences the learner if only by the contagion of the teacher's attitude. Meanwhile, the classroom itself undergoes alteration: the enculturative process defined merely as passive mentation is superseded by analysis, criticism, originality, and participation, with all the modifications in learning and teaching that these processes imply. Like the savage of prehistory who could have learned how to innovate by experimenting with wet mud, so the student of today needs also to get his hands literally dirty. Pottery-making that is not merely imitative but imaginative and creative is, indeed, a symbol of the demand of the progressivist that the school become, first of all, an art studio and science laboratory in active partnership.

One final comment with regard to learning-teaching as a cultural process. It was pointed out in Chapter 4 that this process has intricate relations to the philosophic discipline of epistemology. Viewed afresh in the light of this chapter, the search for truth through education—surely a high responsibility—is differently conceived by the two philosophies to which we have given chief attention. For the essentialist, because truth is already embodied in the nature of the universe and culture, the chief task of the school is to place the learner in a position of receptivity and then to see to it that he acquires as much truth as he possibly can by direct exposure. For the progressivist, truth is not already present, awaiting disclosure; it is always in the making, always unfinished, always subject to correction as learners engage in further interactions with their natural and human environment. To be sure, truth from this viewpoint is not anywhere nearly as complete as essentialism claims that it is. At the same time, such a process of attaining truth invites ceaseless search for more accurate fruitful ways of understanding and directing human and physical experience.

Moreover, the practical significance of progressivist epistemology, if not obvious at first glance, is as far-reaching in its way as the concept of cultural order could be far-reaching in providing new designs for the curriculum. Indeed, perhaps the single most practical service of this view of truth-seeking turns out to be not so much a technique as a contagiously adventuresome approach to the entire learning-teaching process.

The Control of Education and Cultural Goals

Just as we have attempted to relate the problem of the curriculum to cultural order and the problem of teaching-learning to cultural process, so the problem of educational control may be related to cultural goals. As in the other two kinds of relationship, we are, of course, once more selective. Cultural goals actually permeate both the curriculum and the learning-teaching process, while cultural order and process are, in turn, inseparable from the problem of educational control.

Nevertheless, it is fruitful to look at the question of how schools and colleges shall be controlled in the perspective of cultural goals. A chronic weakness in education—particularly in the typical controls over public education—is the too-frequent failure to answer this question forthrightly: What, after all, is the *purpose* of all these rules and regulations? In short, what is education *for*? The busy superintendent of schools, the harrassed principal, the supervisor, the school board member, the college dean—no one of these is likely, unless he happens to be exceptional, to consider as very urgent this most urgent of all questions.

To be sure, almost any superintendent can pull from his filing cabinet some officially authorized statement on the "objectives" of his school system. But logical analysis of its language will almost invariably expose such a welter of undefined platitudinous terms as to render such a statement almost valueless. To write of the need for "well-educated men," of "critical thinking," of "responsible citizenship," and similar goals is motivated by sincere intentions, certainly. It fails, however, to tell us what we most require; it fails to place these generalities in the setting of real cultures through which alone they become meaningful. Indeed, what any controller needs most to know is: Where is our culture going? And, above all: Where *ought* it to go in the future? Then, and only then, can he begin to answer parallel questions for the great enculturative agency he represents.

From our earlier discussion of cultural goals, we recall two major ways of approaching them—the one, cultural relativism; the other, cultural universalism. We saw, too, that anthropologists seem to be moving toward accord that neither of these ways of looking at the goals of culture is sufficient in its use. True, every culture does have its own goals (or, in language closer to axiology, its own value orientation) and in significant respects these are unique to each culture. Equally true, however, is the cross-cultural nature of certain other goals. Michener's *Hawaii*, to which we have referred, dramatizes wonderfully this polarity of relativism *and* universalism. Hawaii is an amalgam of a number of cultures, each of which has contributed something original. Yet at the same time people from the Polynesian, Chinese, Japanese, North American, and other cultures have learned how to live in harmony and to appreciate one another because they have discovered how much at heart they are similar human beings.

From the point of view of educational goals, the bipolar concept of relativism-universalism therefore means that effective
control must be guided, on the one hand, by values that are distinctive to the particular community within which the school operates and, on the other hand, by the wider values of region,
nation, and even the world. A high priority task of the educational leader is to search for and develop a balance of both kinds.

Let us once more illustrate. We assume that an administrator
with a strong background in the nature of culture is more likely
to recognize than he would otherwise that one of the cross-
cultural values of almost, if not completely, planetary scope is
the rich satisfaction that human beings receive from sharing significantly in the operation of those institutions to which they
belong—familial, political, economic, and others. Because of
such recognition, he is accordingly more likely also to work for
the establishment of school or college policies and practices that
provide abundant opportunities for this sort of sharing to occur.

Here, indeed, is the reconstructionist type of approach to the
whole problem of educational control. This philosophy, related
as it is to the science of anthropology, finds that *participation* is a
cross-cultural value which, while not necessarily universal, appears from the evidence to be very widespread. Therefore, ad-
ministrations influenced by this approach are likely to create
every conceivable opportunity for parents to engage in planning
the work of the school, for involving teachers in problems of curriculum and learning, and for including students (beginning at a
very early age) in their own share of cooperative responsibilities.
At the same time, they take into account the cultural habits of
the individual community: thus, a community where a high degree of religious or familial authority has been traditional can
hardly be expected to move as rapidly toward a reconstructed
pattern of control as one that has not.

This is not to say that the culture-oriented leader merely com-
promises between particular situation and projected goal. He
recognizes the need of patience and strategy, of course. But he
also recognizes that, insofar as participation is a common value,

its denial always means that those denied must suffer, consciously or not, from aggressive hostile feelings and behavior that can only damage the well-being of the entire school, and so of the community it serves.

There is, however, another very impressive approach to the problem of cultural goals in relation to educational control—that of the perennialist philosophy. In common with reconstructionism it agrees that much more serious attention should be given the goals of education than is usually given. But the perennialist has a special attitude, rooted as his thinking is in a special set of ontological and other metacultural assumptions. The goals of education—and, indeed, of culture—are for him expressions of the much wider teleological direction of reality as a whole, a direction from the "potential" to the ever more "actual." In a fundamental sense, the business of education is to become as conscious as possible of this unfolding of reality and so to enlist the schools in the everlasting effort to achieve it. And yet, because the ultimate end of culture (for many perennialists, certainly) is not within culture at all, but in the afterlife of salvation and eternity, we discover this to be the great magnetic goal that finally shapes both the order of the curriculum and the central processes of enculturation.

In terms of education control it follows that, unlike reconstructionist theory, perennialist education encourages a strong policy of authority in the hands of those who, by virtue of their higher actualization in the alleged order of reality, are also closer to the goal of education than any other members of a school system—than teachers, for example. Therefore, these leaders are the ones who rightly control school policy and practice.

In all fairness, however, we should mention that not all perennialists, as we have defined them, are quite so directly influenced by a doctrine of such theological intent. As a secular perennialist, Robert M. Hutchins, for example, does not formulate his purposes in the same symbols as those who regard the goal of salvation as the crucial one. Even he, however, suggests the belief that the goals of education (and implicitly of the culture as well) should be discovered and expressed by an intellectual elite. Indeed, in one essay he goes so far as to state forthrightly that only a philosopher-king is worthy to be president of a university at all.

The practical significance of these contrasting theories of educational control lies in the question of whether education can develop an axiological theory that is grounded primarily in anthropological theory and research. If it cannot, then perhaps perennialism is the kind of philosophy to emulate. If, however, it can, then the educational administrator will have to give much more careful attention to the reconstructionist kind of value orientation than he has thus far given.

In Conclusion

Three pervasive questions have been raised:

First, can the curriculum develop greater practical meaning if reinterpreted in the light of cultural order? Our answer has been that it can. Especially on secondary and undergraduate college levels, cultural order is an exciting and fruitful model by which to build integrated designs for general education.

Second, can the teaching-learning process become more integrative and more dynamic in terms of cultural process? Our answer, again, is yes. Both essentialism, with its strong emphasis on conditioning, and progressivism, with its central concern for critical inquiry, help to enrich the process of teaching-learning by placing it in the context of enculturation where, after all, it properly belongs.

Third, can the problem of educational control be clarified when related directly to cultural goals? Two among several important philosophic ways to look at this question are the reconstructionist and the perennialist. The reconstructionist regards the goals of education as determinable primarily by the future-centered goals of culture itself—these, in turn, being delineated through research into the values of people perceived both relatively to their individual cultures and universally in terms of similarities with several or even many cultures. The perennialist insists that, although the goals of education are of great importance, these cannot be determined by culture, as such, but rather by an ontological conception of the universe. This conception centers in a teleological (and often theological) doctrine of the direction of reality toward an inevitable (and often otherworldly) goal. Although both answers are compelling ones, our own preference is for a theory of control grounded in scientific understanding of the goals of humanity on earth. The key challenge to educational leaders is, we believe, to develop policies and programs based squarely upon this kind of understanding.

Recommended Readings for Chapter 5

Barnett, H. G., *Innovation: The Basis of Cultural Change*. New York: McGraw-Hill, 1953.

Brameld, Theodore, *The Remaking of a Culture: Life and Education in Puerto Rico*. New York: Harper & Row, 1959.

Cassirer, Ernst, *An Essay on Man*. New Haven: Yale University Press, 1944; *The Myth of the State*. New Haven: Yale University Press, 1946.

Gruber, Frederick C. (ed.), *Anthropology and Education*. Philadelphia: University of Pennsylvania Press, 1961.

Hegel, G. W. F., *Selections*. New York: Scribner's, 1929.

Heilbroner, Robert, *The Future as History*. New York: Harper & Row, 1960.

Henry, Jules, *Culture Against Man*. New York: Random House, 1963.

Hutchins, Robert M., *The Higher Learning in America*. New Haven: Yale University Press, 1936.

Kahler, Erich, *Man the Measure*. New York: Pantheon, 1943.

Kardiner, Abram, *The Psychological Frontiers of Society*. New York: Columbia University Press, 1945.

Kimball, Solon T., and McClellan, James E., Jr., *Education and the New America*. New York: Random House, 1962.

Kneller, George F., *Educational Anthropology: An Introduction*. New York: Wiley, 1965.

Linton, Ralph, *The Cultural Background of Personality*. New York: Appleton-Century Crofts, 1945.

Muller, Herbert J., *The Uses of the Past*. New York: Oxford University Press, 1952.

Plato, *The Republic*. New York: Scribner's, 1928.

Spengler, Oswald, *The Decline of the West*. New York: Knopf, 1932.

Spindler, George D. (ed.), *Education and Culture*. New York: Holt, Rinehart & Winston, 1963.

Toynbee, Arnold, *A Study of History*. New York: Oxford University Press, 1947, 1956.

Wallace, Anthony F. C., *Culture and Personality*. New York: Random House, 1961.

Whitehead, Alfred N., *The Aims of Education and Other Essays*. New York: Macmillan, 1929.

Whiting, John W. M., and Child, Irvin L., *Child Training and Personality*. New Haven: Yale University Press, 1953.

III

THE EXPLOSIVE IDEA

OF CLASS

6

THE MEANING OF CLASS

According to the model of culture portrayed in Chapter 3, all cultures are characterized by, among other features, spatial relationships on a horizontal plane and on vertical levels. The vertical dimension of spatial order in culture is the dimension upon which we now propose to concentrate by looking at the nature of culture from one angle of vision—that is, in a kind of vertical cross section. In other words, we intend in this section to dissect one important part of culture and to examine it as critically as we can, in the same way that an anatomist may dissect one part of an animal. Therefore, we intend to leave a good deal out that belongs to the total "organism" of culture.

The Influence of Marxian Theory

Now, although the concept of class is not exclusively identified with Karl Marx (indeed, it is acutely treated as far back as Plato and Aristotle), we shall be further selective by concentrating more heavily upon his interpretation than upon any other. The choice is, we think, defensible if only because authorities widely agree that by far the single most powerful contribution to class theory is the Marxian. Many of them begin, at least, with the work of Marx (and of his lifelong collaborator Engels) and then go on from there.

It is, we contend, especially important for teachers in preparation to have some exposure to Marxism, if for no other reason than that they have rarely been exposed to it in their earlier education. Any objective census taken of American students, certainly on the high school level, would show that many are appallingly ignorant not only of the nature of Marxian theory, but of the great political systems that openly declare they are based upon the principles of that theory—namely, the socialist and communist systems that have been spreading across the planet for some fifty years.

But while they are often ignorant through no fault of their own, is it not likely that most students would enjoy the opportunity to become acquainted with Marxian theory—not necessarily because they want to be convinced, but because they know that in the world of today its influence is exceedingly great? Approximately a third of the total population of the world—that is, about one billion people—now live under regimes that are officially based upon Marxism. Moreover, they are taught to believe that here is the one and only true social, political and, if you wish, educational doctrine.

It would be a mistake to say that Marxian theory has made no significant impression even upon our own country. Directly, the Socialist Party, for example, was able some years ago to poll approximately one million votes in a national election. The Communist Party exerted considerable influence in the depression years. More recently, the Socialist Workers Party and the Socialist Labor Party have run presidential and lesser candidates on the ballots of a number of states. Both parties, although relatively small, are militantly and avowedly Marxian.

Indirectly, however, the influence in America of the class concept as interpreted by Marx is certainly much greater. For one thing, it is widely conceded that the small radical parties—especially the Socialist—have often advocated national policies, such as security against old age, that are later incorporated into the platforms of the large parties. For another thing, the filtering-down process has been constant in the realm of ideas, particularly ideas in the social sciences. Take as one example the remark of Charles Beard, one of the most famous American historians, to the effect that Marx was the single greatest intellectual giant of the nineteenth century. That Marxism influenced Beard's economic interpretation of the Constitution, as well as other works of his own and of his many disciples, is indisputable.

But other social scientists have been influenced too. More recently than Beard, for example, C. Wright Mills, a sociologist, made impressive impact upon our understanding of American culture through such works as *White Collar* and *The Power Elite*. Even though modified by intellectual and historical developments that have occurred since Marx and Engels formulated their theory over a century ago, both works have been strongly affected by Marxian thought.

In various other countries outside the Soviet orbit, Marxism has also helped to shape the minds and practices of men. Perhaps the single most influential sociological theorist since Marx has been Max Weber, a German, who modified Marxian concepts but who nevertheless reflected their substantial impact upon him and upon his followers, including Mills. In England, the Labour Party has been guided by leaders some of whom, undoubtedly, have interpreted events through the class concept largely as Marx understood it. In the 1930s and 1940s, the brilliant political thinker Harold J. Laski was a member of the executive committee of the British Labour Party; he was also at one period much read and listened to in the United States. Other powerful intellectuals were G. D. H. Cole and R. H. Tawney. More famous and much admired in our country is George Bernard Shaw, many of whose plays reflect the Marxian orientation and who considered himself a Fabian Socialist during most of his long lifetime. Nor is the impact of Marxian ideas limited to Western countries. In Japan, for example, these ideas have played a significant role among intellectuals and in political life; they continue to do so today.

Dialectical Materialism

The list of followers, some of them with strong reservations, some with almost none, could be extended a long way. But we must turn now to the main features of Marxian theory itself, with special regard, of course, for what it says about the nature of class. The foundation of this theory is called, in the technical language of philosophy, *dialectical materialism*. This term is more comprehensive than "historical materialism," as used in Chapter 4, in that it embraces the entire universe. Historical materialism is more often limited to the human sphere. Some advocates of the latter would not necessarily accept all aspects of dialectical materialism and, therefore, could not be considered Marxists without qualification. In our interpretation, Marxism and dialectical materialism are equivalent terms.

Although sometimes denied by doctrinaire Marxists, dialectical materialism developed directly out of the mainstream of classical philosophy in modern Europe. As a young man, Marx received his doctoral degree in philosophy and, as was customary in the Germany of the first half of the nineteenth century, he came under the spell of the single most powerful thinker of that period, George William Frederick Hegel.

Although the Hegelian philosophy is often abstract and intricate, its key feature is not difficult to grasp. The world, says Hegel, is a spiritual world but it is by no means peaceful and contented. Rather, the world is one of constant change—change, moreover, characterized by a good deal of tension, conflict, and opposition, interspersed by periods of calm and harmony which, although they may succeed in overcoming such disturbances, are followed by a new spiral of change and disequilibrium.

The term "dialectical" in Hegel's philosophy refers to this basic ontological fact of a kind of restless spirituality. His famous formula for the process is *thesis*, *antithesis*, and *synthesis*. It applies to every aspect of reality, psychological as well as material and social. Hegel might have shown that "love" is the "thesis" of human personality, the "antithesis" being "hate," and the "synthesis" being not "love versus hate" but a deeper richer dynamic of human emotion in which both love and hate fuse into a new emotional amalgam and thereby play a normal role within the mature personality. Here, by the way, is one of the points at which the Hegelian philosophy could have influenced the great master of modern psychiatry Sigmund Freud. Freud gives a great deal of attention to the conflicts from which all human beings suffer—conflicts often centering unconsciously in the dialectic of love and hate.

But it was, of course, the dialectic of social change that attracted Marx most. As we shall note more fully in a moment, he found in Hegel the key to the principle that economic classes, too, are in a state of tension and conflict, and yet that they are equally subject to dialectical laws that assure eventual reconciliation and synthesis of the oppositions in them.

To understand this principle more clearly we must first ask: How does "materialism" enter Marx's worldview? He rejected, of course, the idealistic ontology of Hegel and substituted for it an ontology of matter. Reality is not to be understood in terms of spirit or mind, but rather in terms of the events and things of a wholly natural world. In this respect, Marx was already on the side of modern science. As the next chapter will indicate, this does not mean that his philosophy of science is without grave defects. On the contrary, it is in certain ways both obsolete and inconsistent. Nevertheless, it does properly assume that if we are to understand the world scientifically we have to examine facts and processes objectively, subjecting them to empirical observation and explanation. Concepts like "spirit" are unscientific precisely because they cannot thus be tested.

Dialectical materialism, briefly, is that picture of the universe that regards the whole of nature as engaged in an observable and analyzable process of conflict and resolution of conflict. The seriousness with which it is still regarded is dramatized by the fact that if you were now a student in a philosophy of education course in Moscow University, say, you would probably take for granted that your professor is a dialectical materialist and he would take for granted, in turn, that you as a future teacher expect to be if you are not already. This is certainly not to suggest that he and you would necessarily agree at every point; dialectical materialism is by no means as black-and-white as that. Like all powerful philosophies, one of its great attractions is the diversity of meanings it invites within the unity of its framework.

We are better equipped now to turn to the heart of our problem. How, more precisely, does Marxian theory interpret the nature of class? Here we shall borrow again from the concept of culture, by operating with the three familiar dimensions—order, process, goals—as these help to throw light upon and thus give richer meaning to the structures, dynamics, and directions of human beings living together in various forms of cultural arrangement.

The Order of Classes

According to the Marxist, all cultures (except the most primitive) have always been divided into classes. In deliberately naïve terms, let us first say that these classes consist of those people "who have" and those who "have not," with some people in between who may have a little. The class which "has" is also the class that controls; it possesses the authority and power to determine the conditions under which all classes live and work. The class which "has not" is the class without control, and therefore without authority and power. Again in between are those who may have a little control and a little power. This triple pattern applies alike to slave societies, to feudal societies, and to modern societies—also to monarchies, oligarchies, autocracies, and so-called capitalist "democracies."

Marx, of course, was chiefly interested in the class structure of modern industrial culture. In his great three-volume work, *Das Kapital*, he analyzed more meticulously than anyone ever had before him the character of the class relations of this kind of culture. When he writes of *capitalism* (a term he made popular in many languages), he is writing in one way or another of the order of classes in a system distinguished by a particular form of economic activity.

In this kind of economy, the "haves" consist of those who control what Marx called the *means of production*: all the machinery, all the accounting and investment procedure, and all the skills needed to produce goods for a special purpose—namely, profit. The heart of the capitalist system is industrial production to produce profit for the *owning and employing class* that controls the means of production. Here, we obviously anticipate the second cultural category, process, to which we return shortly.

In addition to the class with power to control production in its own primary interest, another class exists to perform the labor needed to produce the products that are sold for profit. This is called the *working class*. It by no means consists exclusively of men and women who wear overalls and who get their hands greasy. It includes many of us who earn our salaries by paperwork or in other kinds of white-collar occupations, but who are still under the control of the employing class. We, too, are considered just as much members of the working class as those who tend machines, fell trees, or perform myriads of other muscular exertions.

Between the powerful minority at the top and the working masses below is a group of people, varying in size from one industrial order to another, which seems, as it were, to have one foot in one class and one foot in the other. This is the *middle class* which Marx sometimes liked to call the *petit bourgeoisie*, the small shopkeepers, farmers, producers, and professionals who succeed in owning a little property or saving enough money out of their earnings to buy a few shares of stock in such great capitalist enterprises as General Motors. These people are not, however, actually members of the controlling class, Marx contends, although they may have illusions that they are. The bulk of shares remains safely in the hands of a small group—the actual center of power that determines company policies for its own maximum gain. In economic reality, therefore, a large proportion of the middle grouping are closer by far to the working class than to the controlling class.

So we see that, according to Marxian theory when reduced to its barest terms, the order of culture in which we presently live is organized into classes characterized primarily in terms of the possession of economic power or its lack of such power. Here is the kind of materialism—that of economic motivation and interest—with which Marx is most concerned.

Classes in Process

The second great dimension of Marxian theory in cultural perspective is the process by which classes engage in dialectical conflict and resolution of conflict. The key terms here are *consciousness* and *struggle*.

How does class consciousness develop? Marx demonstrates that it is a very complicated and even subtle process. Many individuals who work in capitalist enterprises are not in the least aware of their actual class position. They accept their salaries, they spend them, but they never ask themselves, "What is our relationship to the system as a whole? How much control, if any, do we have over it?" These questions may be asked even less frequently by white-collar workers than by so-called blue-collar workers, because the former oftener imagine themselves as sharing some of the same benefits of prestige and authority that the controlling class enjoys.

Nevertheless, Marx contends, some working people of both sorts gradually become critical of the system as a whole and of their own role in maintaining it. As they do so, they begin to become class conscious. They begin to realize that they have a different position in the order of culture from that of the controllers of the instruments of production. And as their class consciousness matures, as they examine the intricate process by which profit is made and distributed, they may become dissatisfied and even aggressively hostile.

What they discover, from the Marxian viewpoint, is deeply disturbing to their sense of justice. A man works so many hours a day to produce, let us say, a pair of shoes. He is paid $6 for the labor he expends. But the man who controls the instruments of production, after paying all the expenses and taxes involved, sells the pair of shoes for $7. The difference between what the worker receives in wages and the price the controller is able to demand for them is called *surplus value*—a term connoting that the worker in effect contributes part of his labor free of charge. Otherwise, he would have received $7 in wages.

The process is, of course, much more involved as Marx describes it, but for our purpose the point is clear enough. As class consciousness develops, the worker asks himself, "Is this fair? Is it reasonable that each day I should work an hour or more for which I am not actually paid?" At the same time, he may become aware not only of strictly economic deprivation, but of psychological concomitants such as lack of participation in the rules of work, separation from the product he helps to make, and so a kind of emotional dualism which Marx calls "alienation"—a term that has become recently influential in social psychology.

Such awareness, however, also stimulates him to talk with other workers who are thinking along similar lines. Eventually they decide to join in some kind of common agreement that the profit-making process is wrong because it is exploitative—that is, it takes advantage of the worker's weakness, his lack of power and authority, in order to benefit a class that decides what proportion of his labor he shall be paid for. Here is the root of his discontent that eventually leads to the organization of *trade unions*. From a Marxian viewpoint, a union is nothing more nor less than a group of class-conscious workers who have united to protect, regulate, and obtain what they consider to be a fair share of the economic fruits of the industrial system. The union is, in a sense, the most fundamental of all economic institutions concerned with dialectical change, for it is chiefly through this organized means that the worker is able to develop control.

Thus, we return to the question of power. Earlier it was noted that, according to Marxian theory, economic power has been located primarily in the hands of those who own and control the instruments of production. But since workers lack this kind of power, is it possible for them to develop any kind at all? There is only one answer: workers do possess another kind, the power of their own labor and their willingness or lack of willingness to sell it to employers in exchange for wages. They cannot, however, exercise this power single-handedly. Should an individual worker declare his unwillingness to work for a given wage, he is simply dismissed and replaced by another willing one, of whom there are usually a great many. The only recourse, accordingly, is the unity of common organization to which all workers belong and by whose policies they agree to abide. It follows that the power of workers does not center in the instruments of production, as such, but in what Marx calls their organized *labor power*. If they are collectively strong enough they can refuse to work unless their terms of remuneration, hours, security, and other protections against exploitation are met. Thus, we can understand why, in Marx's terms, the *strike* is the supreme weapon of the working class. By denying the employer labor power, it blocks the source of vitality upon which capitalism depends for its existence—the source of surplus value itself.

We find ourselves now confronting the aspect of the class process, namely, struggle. For, as workers unite and form powerful trade unions (and, we might add, political parties based upon labor organizations, such as the British Labour Party or the Japanese Socialist Party) they challenge the power of the controllers to have their own way.

The processes by which the struggle manifests itself are, however, many. Thus, what is now termed "collective bargaining" is the technique by which workers and employers try, by meeting together around a common table, to reach agreement as to the rules by which the former will sell their labor power and the latter will pay for it. Often, this process works well enough to prevent a work stoppage, but when it does not do so the union representatives may call a strike. Then there is always the possibility of violence instigated by one side or the other, or perhaps by both.

Of course, as Marx points out, class consciousness develops on both sides—increasingly so as the struggle intensifies. As the controlling class becomes more sharply aware of its own stake in the system, it too develops a variety of techniques for maintain-

ing its power. It forms its own organizations. It selects and fi-
nances political candidates—in fact, it builds great political parties, such as the Republican Party in the United States. With its
vast financial resources it is also able to influence public opinion
in its favor through ownership of newspapers and other agencies
of communication. It tries to reach into classrooms by providing
propaganda material to school libraries and teachers. Sometimes, if it sees its power seriously threatened by the growth and
militancy of the working people, it resorts to extreme measures
of oppression, such as moving its factories to another part of the
country where labor organization is weak. It may even persuade
the police to destroy a strike by the use of force.

Often, however, such measures only serve to intensify the opposition. Labor, too, learns how to propagandize, how to build
political strength, and how to meet force with force. The result is
that, according to Marxian theory, the dialectic of thesis (the ruling class) and antithesis (the working class) reaches a stage of
such acute tension that only a new synthesis will serve to resolve
the conflicts that recur at intervals because they are inherent in
the very structure of capitalism. Sometimes this means a violent
breaking point: nothing less than civil war (as in China or Cuba)
or even international war (which Marxists insist are at bottom
economic in cause, such as violent struggles for control of natural resources). This is the stage of *revolution*.

Although we may define revolution as thoroughgoing social
and cultural change, it does not necessarily follow that every revolution is accompanied by violence. In countries where democratic and parliamentary machinery is sufficiently strong and
flexible, revolution may be achieved, says Marx, through legal
and educational processes—a hope of the American Socialists,
among other parties influenced by Marxism. Where violence
cannot be averted, or even where it is seriously threatened by
counterforces, the working people will have to take over the government themselves and strictly control the opposition—a device called the "dictatorship of the proletariat," which Marx
briefly formulated and Lenin elaborated. It was Stalin, however,

who gave the term worldwide notoriety: his dictatorship, which he rationalized in accordance with Marxian theory, was characterized by many years of suppression and liquidation of his enemies. The extent to which some of his successors have modified his own extremism is not yet determined with any precision, although it is apparently large in the "iron curtain" countries, including the Soviet Union itself.

The Goal: A Classless Society

Theoretically, the dictatorship of the proletariat is only a temporary means to the goal of a social order in which class conflict is replaced by class cooperation. This is, of course, the core meaning of a Communist or Socialist society. Some interesting distinctions between these two societies have been made by the Marxian philosophers, but we shall not trouble with them here. The important term is *classless society*. It is, for the Marxist, the supreme goal of historical evolution—the synthesis that justifies all the agonies of class struggle both within industrial nations and among them. What does the classless society actually mean?

Although Marx said relatively little about it, we can agree that he refers to a socioeconomic order in which one class no longer exploits another class through ownership of the instruments of production. Because by definition a class is a group of people who either control or are controlled by the instruments of production, one class, in a sense, always begets another class. The employing class under capitalism literally creates the working class, yet without the latter the former could not exist either. Thus, if we change the system so that neither depends upon the other, we thereby destroy classes themselves. The conclusion logically follows from the definitions in the premises.

Today, the goal that millions of followers of Marx want to achieve is a world society where the worker, who expends his physical and mental energies in producing the goods that are necessary to civilized life, also controls the instruments that produce them. Actually, if Marxists are correct, precedents may be found for this kind of system within contemporary capitalist orders. Wherever an enterprise is owned and controlled by the people—where, accordingly the controllers are not a group who siphon off profits but are the full beneficiaries of the labor power they exert—you already have the rudiments of a classless society. For instance, in the Tennessee Valley Authority (TVA) electric power is generated by the Tennessee River and its tributaries and is sold at a much lower rate than in most parts of the United States. The central reason is that the people own the rivers and the dams and the power that is generated is also publicly owned. True, it is sold to communities which may, in turn, make a profit, but so far as the power itself is concerned it is, in principle, a symbol of socialism. The post office is another example: nobody makes a profit from distributing letters, although it would be perfectly possible to turn it into a private enterprise, just as are such noncompetitive services as the telegraph and telephone systems in the United States. Public schools are still another example: they are not conducted in order that private owners may profit from the labor that teachers perform.

What the present-day Marxist wants is to universalize this kind of piecemeal situation until eventually no profit-making enterprises remain. He would, for instance, transform the great private corporations, such as General Electric, into public corporations owned by the people so that the full fruits of their labor power would be returned to them in goods and services. Many democratic countries have gone further in this direction than has our own. In England and in the Scandinavian countries, public utilities are genuinely public in both ownership and authority. New Zealand is an example of a country in which medical and health services are largely under public control. Even in Puerto Rico, a United States commonwealth, all public utilities except the telephone are owned by the people; yet Puerto Rico in many other respects is not a socialist society.

While the cultural goal of classlessness, then, is the target of history for the Marxist, this does not mean that for him people are sometime going to be all alike. Talents, interests, personalities, the great range of skills and services needed in any modern civilization, guarantee that wide differences will remain—perhaps will even increase—as the destructive effects of exploitation diminish and finally disappear.

Likewise, for the Marxist, the classless society does not mean that you cannot own a home or a garden or an automobile. Private property is perfectly consistent with a socialist order, provided that such private property is for personal use and does not produce a profit for the person who owns it. If one cultivates his private garden, let him grow all the vegetables he wants, but don't let him sell the vegetables at a profit by hiring gardeners and extracting surplus value from their labor power.

The classless society is epitomized by this famous definition: it is a society in which each produces according to his abilities and receives according to his needs. But abilities and needs vary enormously. Thus, the Marxian goal is one that envisages a wide range of individual differences within a common, public, socialized order run by the people themselves.

To be sure, says the Marxist, the bitter hostility of the controlling groups may for a long time block or retard the achievement of this goal. Also, the nations still under capitalist rule may precipitate conflict not only within but between nations. Indeed, a contention of Soviet leaders, reiterated ever since the Revolution of 1917, is that their dictatorship, including strong military defense, is forced upon them by the continuous harrassment of hostile powers. More recently, this has been even more militantly the position of Communist China. Nevertheless, the ultimate goal for Marxists everywhere remains the same—a *worldwide* classless society.

Critical Reaction to the Class Idea

We summarize up to this point. The meaning of class has been developed by operating further with the cultural dimensions of order, process, and goals studied in Part II. The *order* of classes for Marxian theory is determined primarily by the structure and locus of economic power. The *process* of classes centers in the emergence of class consciousness, while class struggle is the overt expression of such consciousness. Finally, the highest *goal* of this dialectical process is the establishment of a classless society in which exploitation or control of one class by another is supplanted by public power in the hands of those whose physical and mental energies produce the consumable goods of earth and industry.

Hundreds of questions have been raised about Marxian theory, ranging all the way from bitter repudiation to friendly modification. The whole concept of class has been subjected to a vast amount of discussion and research. This is true even in the United States, where class consciousness and struggle have been less overt than in many countries—less overt for various complex reasons, only one of which is a traditional distaste for class hierarchies based upon invidious feelings of higher and lower rank. Currently, social scientists shy away from Marxian terminology. A good example is the "inventory of scientific findings," *Human Behavior*, by Bernard Berelson and Gary A. Steiner. The term "class struggle" is found only once in the section on "social conflict," yet this entire section is easily interpreted in terms consistent with Marxism. The latter term is not in the index.

Orthodox Marxian theory has also been modified in varying degrees by both Marxists and by non-Marxists. The most influential Marxist since Marx and Engels was unquestionably Nikolai Lenin, the great leader of the Russian Revolution. We shall see in the following chapter that Lenin was something of a philosopher as well as a practical revolutionary leader. Perhaps his most famous supplementation of Marxism, however, is his refinement of the political theory that the *state* is always an instrument of class power—that even in a "democracy" like our own, the legislature, courts, and military are overt or covert allies of the dominant class. The dictatorship of the proletariat is thus also a state; this time, however, the class in control has shifted to the working people. When such control is no longer needed because opposition has been replaced by general support, then the state, by definition, "withers away." Because its coercive role has ended, its own usefulness has also ended. Only public services under governmental direction are still needed, such as health agencies, roads, schools, and a multitude of other services that every modern society requires in order to function efficiently and beneficially.

Many non-Marxists or pseudo-Marxists have also sought to correct the class theory as Marx formulated it. Take one rather typical recent work, Ralf Dahrendorf's *Class and Class Conflict in Industrial Society*. This German-born sociologist tries to prove that Marxian theories have been largely outmoded by technological and other historical changes. He notes, for example, the tremendous growth of the middle classes, which seem to have blunted the class struggle in countries like the United States: here even organized labor is much more concerned to share in high profits and in the affluence of home ownership or the latest electrical gadgets than to organize for political power leading to social ownership of the instruments of production. Again, he points out how social mobility rather than rigidity of class divisions seems to be occurring in a way that affords more opportunity to climb from one class to another than Marx predicted.

Dahrendorf also reviews such recent class studies as that of Milovan Djilas, the famous Yugoslav theorist who was imprisoned for contending in books such as *The New Class* that a new ruling elite is developing in Communist states—a minority whose vast power and privilege lie no longer in private ownership of the instruments of production but in control of the Communist Party apparatus and, through this, of the collectivized technology.

We must confine ourselves to but one other controversial treatment—the influential theory and research of the American social anthropologist W. Lloyd Warner and his associates. Warner looks at social stratification in terms of what he calls "status"— this being determined by the degree of prestige or lack of prestige that a person acquires in a given community according to the judgment of his fellow citizens. In the communities he studied firsthand, Warner usually found six status levels called, in his terminology, the upper-upper, lower-upper, upper-middle, lower-middle, upper-lower, and lower-lower. These six levels are not necessarily prevalent in all communities of the country, but they are prevalent in many.

Warner contends that economic position, while important, is by no means as sufficient in explaining a person's social status as Marxists have tended to believe. The upper-upper level, for example, consists of old aristocratic families of the community, not necessarily the richest. The lower-uppers may be much richer than the upper-uppers, but the upper-uppers have more prestige and in many ways more influence.

Recent literature on social stratification and class structure reveals almost as much skepticism concerning the validity of Warner's methods of research, the adequacy of his theory, and the reliability of his findings, as toward those of Marx. Students are urged to examine some of this literature in our recommended readings. We cite again only an instance: Kurt B. Mayer's *Class and Society*—a brief but superb overview of the class problem as it applies to American culture. Mayer contends that class and status should not be confused: a person may develop all kinds of psychological notions about his own prestige or that of others which could be at odds with his actual class position in the sense of economic control or lack of control. Indeed, many Americans seem to have no clear consciousness of their class position—one consequence of which is their lack of sophisticated understanding of the power structure or of their own role in coping with it. If Mayer is correct, then Warner has failed to appreciate the relevance of Marxian theory for American culture. Mayer himself, however, hastens to add that our culture is in many respects different from the kind Marx knew in his time or predicted for ours. Like Dahrendorf and others, he calls attention to the high rate of social mobility in American culture and to the growth of the middle classes—both of which, among many other factors, mitigate against the Marxian strategy of social and political change. Nevertheless, Mayer would probably agree with Ruth R. Kornhauser's critical analysis of the Warner approach when she states that various social scientists do not find this approach to be a "disconfirmation of the Marxian view of class or of the so-called 'economic interpretation' of class in general."*

Were space available we should like to go much further with elaborations and criticisms. If it is true, for example, that we are tending toward a middle-class culture, that instead of moving toward sharper and sharper dialectical polarities of the upper and the lower classes, we have moved increasingly toward a diffusion of classes, does this necessarily mean that power and control have also shifted toward the broad middle groups? This question, like most others in class theory, finds different answers in different quarters. Surely, however, it does seem true that the middle levels play a very important role; indeed, a case could be made to the effect that they have decided recent national elections in the United States by holding the balance of economic and hence political power.

The growth of the middle classes generates other exciting questions. One of these, as Max Lerner, in *America as a Civilization*, and others have shown, is a trend toward conformity, an overemphasis on status-seeking and on the habits of "conspicuous consumption," which Thorstein Veblen so caustically exposed well over a generation ago in his famous *Theory of the Leisure Class*. Since then, Vance Packard has popularized similar views in *The Status Seekers* and other books.

In any case, despite the breathtaking speed with which the processes of culture have moved since Marx and Engels exploded their class idea in the rather unwilling ears of the world, no one can deny that this idea still holds tremendous fascination. As mentioned at the outset of the chapter, let us remember that

---

*Ruth R. Kornhauser, in Reinhard Bendix and Seymour M. Lipset (eds.), *Class, Structure and Power* (Glencoe: Free Press, 1953), pp. 245–46.

dialectical materialism is still spreading its philosophic influence, especially in parts of the world where middle classes are the exception rather than the rule, and where the common people are ruthlessly disenfranchised, exploited, and oppressed. One of the greatest challenges to America lies in this fact. Unless we wish simply to turn our backs upon it or to treat these vast millions as our enemies—neither of which most of us wish to do—we shall have to ask whether there are not meanings, both positive and negative, in the continued appeal of Marxian theory that we Americans will have to take into serious account. Perhaps, as we move to the next two chapters, there is even opportunity to achieve a new synthesis—a synthesis that would incorporate some of the insights and tools of this theory into a contemporary modernized approach to the class problem and to the responsibility of education in coping with it.

Recommended Readings for Chapter 6

Beard, Charles, *The Economic Interpretation of the Constitution of the United States*. New York: Macmillan, 1913.

Berelson, Bernard, and Steiner, Gary A., "Social Conflict," in *Human Behavior: An Inventory of Scientific Findings*. New York: Harcourt, Brace & World, 1964.

Cole, G. D. H., *What Marx Really Meant*. New York: Knopf, 1934.

Dahrendorf, Ralf, *Class and Class Conflict in Industrial Society*. Stanford: Stanford University Press, 1959.

Djilas, Milovan, *The New Class*. New York: Praeger, 1957.

Feuer, Lewis (ed.), *Marx and Engels: Basic Writings on Politics and Philosophy*. New York: Doubleday, 1959.

Fromm, Erich, *Marx's Concept of Man*. New York: Ungar, 1961.

Hegel, G. W. F., *Selections*. New York: Scribner's, 1929.

Kornhauser, Ruth R., in Bendix, Reinhard, and Lipset, Seymour M. (eds.), *Class, Status and Power*. Glencoe: Free Press, 1953.

Laski, Harold J., *The American Democracy*. New York: Viking, 1948.

Lenin, Nikolai, *State and Revolution*. London: British Socialist Party, 1919.

Lerner, Max, *America as a Civilization*. New York: Simon and Schuster, 1957.

Marx, Karl, *Capital and Other Writings* (with F. Engels and N. Lenin). New York: Modern Library, 1932.

Mayer, Kurt, *Class and Society*. New York: Random House, 1955.

Mills, C. Wright, *The Power Elite*. New York: Oxford University Press, 1956; *White Collar*. New York: Oxford University Press, 1951.

Packard, Vance *The Status Seekers*. New York: McKay, 1959; *The Hidden Persuaders*. New York: Pocket Books, 1963.

Selsam, Howard, and Martel, Harry (eds.), *Reader in Marxist Philosophy*. New York: International Publishers, 1963.

Shaw, George Bernard, *Fabian Essays in Socialism*. London: Allen and Unwin, 1950.

Tawney, R. H., *Religion and the Rise of Capitalism*. New York: Harcourt, Brace & World, 1926.

Veblen, Thorstein, *The Theory of the Leisure Class*. New York: Macmillan, 1899.

Warner, W. Lloyd, *Social Class in America*. Chicago: Science Research Associates, 1949.

Weber, Max, *The Protestant Ethic and the Spirit of Capitalism*. New York: Scribner's, 1930.

7

PHILOSOPHIC INTERPRETATIONS OF CLASS

View of the Problem

This is the second step in our triple approach to the idea of class. We now ask the question: What can we learn about its meaning if we view it through philosophic lenses? As in the case of culture, we quickly perceive that not just one set of lenses is available but several, depending upon the complex of beliefs out of which each set is constructed.

At this point, perhaps we should reiterate how cumulative is the understanding of the great ideas that this book is exploring. It is never a question of knowing all about any one of the three ideas, for this is impossible even for the greatest authorities; it is always a question, rather, of increasing the degree of understanding a little at a time. To realize that our learning experience is cumulative should reduce frustrations and strengthen our assurance that the real test of success in this exploration lies in the extent to which we feel a sense of increasing significance as to how these ideas *make a difference*, not only in our intellectual development but in our personal and social as well as professional behavior.

Apply this observation to our study of class. The preceding chapter noted that the class structure is an important dimension of what was called, in a still earlier chapter, the "spatial order of culture." That is, cultures always reveal human relationships in vertical layers or strata. By now, this dimension should have become more meaningful. With the help of Marx and other daring explorers in the realm of the class concept, we are better able to appreciate how pervasively every culture is characterized by verticality even when its members fail to recognize, as they often do, their respective positions in particular stratified orders.

Cumulative learning should occur again as we turn to two clusters of philosophic ideas with which we have also had some previous contact: first, the concepts of hypostatization and operationalism; second, the group of educational philosophies to which we have attached such labels as perennialism and essentialism. The chief objective of this chapter is to vitalize further the significance of class by means of these two clusters—both of them, of course, selected from a much larger range of opportunities.

Class: Hypostatic Versus Operational

Let us review for another moment. We remember from Chapter 5 that hypostatization means the practice of objectifying or reifying an idea into a thing. This is the method of magic that the primitive savage uses when he hates somebody and wants to destroy him: he utters a word that he believes will cast a spell on an enemy and thereby injure or destroy him. The people of Salem, Massachusetts, believed that witches could perform this kind of magic. In attaching the word "witch" to a "bedeviled" citizen of the town they, too, performed magic. For the word itself had the power to destroy as effectively as poison.

This crude method of hypostatizing has been clearly explained by one of the greatest philosophers of our century, Ernst Cassirer. It is, he says, characteristic of the symbolic life of primitive cultures down to the present day. But it is not limited to them. It also occurs in modern civilizations whenever philosophers, for example, project one of their concepts into a kind of objective entity, even into an eternally existent thing. Similarly, certain of the great religions attach objective, supernatural powers to some of their symbols: insofar as the pronouncement of certain sacred words is in itself supposed to change the character of a person or event, they, too, have hypostatized.

The operational approach, by contrast, considers ideas to be abstractions *from* experience rather than projections *upon* experience—ideas that are then tested for the difference they make *in* experience. Thus, we have found that the concept of culture can be interpreted as an operational device that scientists of man have created from observing certain ways in which he behaves—ways that are sufficiently different from any others as to require different explanatory principles. Such behavior is not explicable by concepts derived from, say, observations of merely psychological or even sociological behavior. By operating with the culture concept upon the type of human experience that is singled out, the latter acquires additional meaning. Thereby, in turn, opportunities for control often arise that enable the experience itself to be modified.

This is what may happen when an anthropologist studies the cultural patterns of, say, the family. In operating upon these patterns with his conceptual and observational instruments he may eventually reach the point even of being able to affect them in some way. It is only fair to say that the anthropologist's influence is still very meager in bringing about cultural innovation by comparison with other less deliberative influences—such as the often raw crude forces of economic or political action. Here, indeed, a great array of opportunities appears for projects in "applied anthropology"—a relatively new field concerned with the application of cultural concepts to practical issues.

Does the concept of class likewise take on fresh significance if we approach it, on the one hand, from a hypostatic viewpoint and, on the other hand, from an operational viewpoint?

One provocative answer to this question is by way of the fascinating philosophy of dialectical materialism. Our interpretation centers in the thesis that this remarkable theory is an amalgam of both the hypostatic and operational approaches to the nature of class. We shall better understand why both approaches intertwine if we look for a moment at the history of Marxism and the traditions out of which it grew. Chapter 6 reminded us that dialectical materialism tries to join Hegel's dialectic of conflict together with the materialistic view that man's ideas are derived from the external facts of worldly experience—particularly from such economic facts as making a living. Although interested in all aspects of human life, it was, indeed, economic realities in which Marx was most interested when he talked about the materialistic basis of social experience.

Now, Hegelianism, we also remember, developed into a wonderful speculative ontological system. This system extended all the way from inanimate nature, to the individual, to the political state, and ultimately to the universe itself. Moreover, the dialectical process, although one of endless conflicts interspersed with temporary periods of calm, has definite direction and purpose that are themselves inherent in the nature of reality.

Marx took over much of this sweeping conception of reality from Hegel. True, instead of calling the universe spiritual, as Hegel did, he called it material. But he did not repudiate the Hegelian assumption that the universe is governed by objective laws and that these laws guarantee the course of history from stage to stage toward a kind of grand culmination. For Marx, this course led eventually to the downfall of the capitalist controller of the instruments of production, and to the victory of those who operate these instruments—that is, the working people. Such a victory can only mean that the goal of history is a society governed entirely by working people, blue-collar and white-collar, skilled mechanics and professionals, ditchdiggers and scholars.

To understand further the materialistic basis of this grand-scale dialectical order, it is interesting to refer to Lenin's curious work in epistemology. Although Lenin was, first of all, a man of practice—certainly he was not a professional philosopher—he always insisted that without a clear philosophy any program of political action is worthless. While exiled from Czarist Russia, he zealously studied philosophy in the reading room of the British Library and wrote an extraordinary book, *Materialism and Empirio-Criticism*, in which he tried to show that ideas are *epiphenomena*—that is, pictures of the outside materialistic world.

This thesis he held to be of crucial importance in accordance with the Marxian view that ideas about morals, religion, politics, art, or education are primarily the epiphenomena of the prevailing economic order of society and of the power structure undergirding that order.

By joining this conception of truth, as the reflection of an objective reality, to the dialectic of a dynamic universe, dialectical materialism emerges as one of the most comprehensive worldviews in history. Moreover, class becomes an integral part of the whole picture—in many ways the most crucial concept. The main purpose of the entire theory is to explain why classes exist as dialectical stages of social evolution, why struggle between them is inevitable, and why resolution of the struggle eventuates in a new orderly arrangement—a new social synthesis.

The crucial point for our present interest is that classes are treated as objective realities ordained by laws of nature. Thus, they are part and parcel of the hypostatized structure that Marx inherited from Hegel and adapted to his own ends.

Class is not, in this context, primarily a conceptual device by which certain kinds of human relations are explained and directed in contrast to other kinds; indeed, according to Lenin's epistemology, such an interpretation of class is a vicious example of the very theory his book attacks—namely, the theory of idealism that gives to ideas a spurious authority and reality of their own. The only sense for him in which class is legitimately an idea at all is that it is the picture of a prior fact—the fact of an objective reality of inevitable conflict between opposing economic forces. Class is inherent in the dialectic of history itself.

But Lenin, fortunately for the Russian Revolution, was not just an amateur epistemologist; he was a superlative tactican of political strategy. Or, in the language of this discussion, he did not treat the problem of classes merely as a hypostatic system but also, and even more tellingly, as an operationalist would treat it. For this second way, Lenin could also find a good deal of support in the writings of Marx, just as he could for the first. That is to say, Marx, while he never escaped the influence of Hegel's hypostatized absolutism, was too much a man of the mid-nineteenth century not to be aware, or at least partially aware, that there is another, newer, more audacious approach to the great problems of nature and human nature than that of traditional philosophy, still rooted as it was in magical habits of thinking and acting even when cloaked in sophisticated language. This newer approach was grounded in a belief that man does have something very important to say and to accomplish through his own intelligent and collective strength. Here is the revolutionary import of Marx's famous dictum that *man makes history, history does not make man*. In its intent, this dictum is also operational. It is supported by many other statements of similar intent not only in Marx himself but in Engels, Lenin, and other great leaders of the same movement. Here is one example: man "of his own accord," says Marx, "starts, regulates, and controls the material reactions between himself and Nature. . . . By thus acting on the external world and changing it, he at the same time changes his own nature." Here is an example from Lenin: "Human practice must enter into our full definition of a thing, both as criterion of truth, and as practical determiner of its connection with what is needful to mankind."*

So many similar implications may be found in Marxian literature that some interpreters have tried to translate Marx's theory of classes almost entirely into operational terms—that is, into a program for analyzing the great conflicts of modern industrial life and offering a strategy of correction for the chronic evils of the present economic-political order. Operationally, the concept of class may also be used to clarify many problems of an industrial society, such as our own, without necessarily drawing Marx's conclusions that only a radical change will cure its evils. The New Deal period in America, for example, favored greater power and rights for the trade union because liberal leaders hold that the working people as a class had too long been exploited by

---

*As quoted in Theodore Brameld, *A Philosophic Approach to Communism* (Chicago: University of Chicago Press, 1933), pp. 162, 165.

the owning and managerial class. But the improvements the New Deal favored were to occur *within* the capitalist system.

Thus, it is sometimes argued that Marx was a social scientist in the pragmatic sense. He used ideas—the idea of class, above all—to diagnose the social evils of industrial civilization and then to move on to prognoses with appropriate implementation. Lenin has even been called the social engineer of the class struggle—a "revolutionary engineer" who wanted to perform major renovations upon the medieval, autocratic class structure that prevailed in Russia up to 1917.

But this view of Marxian theory is quite as one-sided as an exclusively hypostatic interpretation. The ever-fascinating character of Marxism is due in large part to the fact that you can interpret it either way, depending upon what emphasis you select in terms of what your own premises and interests happen to be. Class can be considered hypostatically or operationally, or both ways alternately, without necessarily realizing the significance of the shift. But confusions are sure to occur unless you do realize which of the ways you are utilizing.

Philosophers in Communist countries have, to a great extent, interpreted Marxism as a universal predetermined system, In this respect, although they deny it, dialectic materialism has developed affinities with the great religions that also hypostatize *their* special systems of symbols. People who accept these systems often come to worship them as having a kind of transcendental power of their own—a power to be acquiesced in, a power for which one may lay down his life, a power which becomes an overwhelming, captivating faith. One of the reasons why ecclesiastic perennialists have always so bitterly opposed dialectical materialism, we suspect, is partly at least because they detect in it the competition of a potent counterreligion—and thus a formidable threat to their own.

We do not here attempt to adjudge one kind of hypostatized system as better than another. We are merely saying that in the almost hypnotic power that dialectical materialism possesses over millions of its devotees, assuring them as it does that they are on the side of destiny and that the ultimate goal of a classless society will eventually occur, certain parallels with several great religious systems are too patent to ignore.

Let us summarize what we have tried to say so far about the hypostatic and operational approaches to the idea of class. The former approach treats class as an objective entity, at least until such time as it is absorbed by a "higher" social order in which all classes, as defined, disappear. Moreover, you and I, inescapably if often still vaguely and intermittently, flow with the mainstream of dialectical evolution and revolution. Thus we cannot avoid being sucked sooner or later into the whirlpool of class conflict, for such is a law of the materialistic universe.

But we have found that some of the ideas of Marx can be utilized operationally, too—for instance, his prescriptions for social action by way of class consciousness and class struggle in order to alleviate the evils of class power. In these respects, we may conceivably learn to function with the concept of class upon our culture so as to provide more meaning *for* culture and even to act upon it in such ways as to try to effect fundamental changes in the vertical order.

Philosophies of Education: The Role of Class

Some of the implications in our discussion thus far should become clearer as we turn to this question: How do contemporary philosophies of education reflect the idea of class and how does the idea of class directly or indirectly influence these philosophies in turn?

To venture a somewhat oversimplified generalization (for there are always qualifications and exceptions), perennialism and essentialism tend to hypostatize their beliefs about class, just as they do about culture. That is to say, they objectify the concept into a reality. However, the continuum of progressivism and reconstructionism tends to take an operational approach. The word "tend" should not be overlooked, however. Undoubtedly, within the perennialist and essentialist camps one will find some proponents who concede a place for operational practices, at least within limits. Similarly, some advocates within the progressivist and reconstructionist camps may reveal hypostatic attitudes. On the whole, nevertheless, the perennialist and essentialist theories tend to look at the world, including its class structure, as an objective preestablished harmony of law and order, whereas the progressivist and reconstructionist are inclined to view the universe as an opportunity to learn how men may engage more and more effectively in the practice of explaining and controlling their world through human struggle and planned ingenuity.

Keeping these two large frames of reference in mind—how more precisely do philosophies of education interpret the idea of class? To begin with perennialism, we are now compelled to note another important aspect of its ontology. Perennialism is based upon a belief that is fundamental to all its others—namely, that *the universe is engaged in an endless process of unfolding* (sometimes termed "actualizing") *from the potentiality of matter to the actuality of form.*

Let us attempt to clarify these abstract terms. Inherent in the very structure of reality are the eternal forms of nature—for example, the forms of flowers or animals—but these are often buried, as it were, in the substrata of undeveloped layers of mud and rock. Some have reached the level of living reality; others have not. The same principle applies to the high level of human reality. Here, too, man possesses great potentialities for the achievement of truth or beauty or goodness, but more often than not this capacity lies sluggish and unrealized. Only occasionally does a breakthrough occur.

From this ontological viewpoint, how would a perennialist be likely to approach the meaning of class? He sees modern culture—indeed, all culture—as one manifestation of this same universal unfolding of potentialities toward more and more actualization or realization of them. This inherent process means that some human beings manage to overcome their lower material natures sufficiently to achieve a degree of spirituality in which reason triumphs over ignorance, beauty over ugliness, goodness over evil. Those who do attain such purity of form are, of course, the masters of virtue and wisdom; it is these who therefore constitute the upper class of any properly organized social order.

Thus, the perennialist ontology provides a rationale for the direction of society and culture toward rule by a spiritual-intellectual elite, with other classes scaled below it according to their several degrees of imperfect actualization. We return to this point in the next chapter, so we shall only add now that, in our judgment, here is the key to understanding some perennialists who are presently influential in American education. They believe that the solution to our educational problems will not be discovered until "virtuous" leaders have emerged who can lead the rest of us toward the pure light of rationality. Because such leaders are always a minority, the perennialist policy, notwithstanding protestations to the contrary, endorses an aristocratic class structure. It is a class structure similar in major respects to that of Plato who, in *The Republic*, conceived the ideal political order to be made up of classes with the rational few (the philosopher-kings) at the top, slaves at the bottom (contemporary perennialists do not, of course, follow Plato here), and artisans and military personnel between.

What about the essentialist's approach to class structure? He agrees with the perennialist that such a structure is inherent in the very laws of reality. Whereas, however, the perennialist is likely to be critical of the prevailing class structure insofar as it may perpetuate mediocrity, the essentialist orientation is more often toward acceptance. After all, the laws of nature and the laws of society ordain the already given order. This belief, by the way, anticipates the doctrine of "social Darwinism" which we consider in our discussion of evolution—a doctrine holding that the class which actually rules is likely to be the class which also ought to rule because it is the fittest, as proved by the laws of economic competition.

The essentialist, therefore, is likely to affirm that education should provide opportunity to study the class structure in order to reflect it clearly in our minds. Thereby we may learn how to follow and obey it. Just as culture is "out there," objectively real, so too is the class structure "out there," objectively real. The primary business of the student is to learn the laws of this already given, class-structured society in order to accept and transmit them.

A telling example of how the essentialist becomes an enculturator concerned primarily to preserve the class structure is to be found in the historical school of modern classical economics from Adam Smith onward. This school provided the theoretical basis of capitalism. To a considerable extent, it is still taken for granted in the economic teachings of typical high schools and colleges. Such laws as supply and demand, it holds, are so necessary and irrevocable that if you want capitalism to work well, you not only have to understand these laws but to obey them. At your peril, do not tamper with them. To do so is only to invite all kinds of trouble. This is typical of the conservative thinking of such contemporary students of capitalism as F. A. Hayek, who has brilliantly attacked the "welfare state" of the New Deal period in America and of the Scandinavian countries as contrary to the laws of class competition and authority.

In education itself, we may mention Conant again as an exemplar of the essentialist approach. Although he rarely talks directly of the class problem, his general attitude is sufficiently revealed by this statement from *Education In a Divided World*: "Granted private ownership and the profit motive (which have been sneered at in certain circles, but for which I believe there is no substitute for this nation), the question [is] how best to keep our society truly competitive and moving toward a greater degree of equality of opportunity. . . .*

Here is one of the beliefs permeating all of Conant's proposals for the public school. Although he rarely articulates his own assumptions as forcibly as in this statement, he is, we contend, an

---

*James B. Conant, *Education in a Divided World* (Cambridge: Harvard University Press, 1948), p. 30.

essentialist conservator. He believes, on the whole, that the school should be used to preserve rather than alter the economic and political system—and thus the class structure indigenous to it. When one hears principals of high schools holding up Conant's studies as models for their own institutions, one should remember that this is another way of saying that they, too, are at least unwitting essentialists. That is, they are leaders who, whether they deliberately intend to or not, support the kind of schools that help to perpetuate the prevailing class system, with all that this entails by way of economic power and economic subservience to a particular kind of economic order. We shall have more to say on this theme when we discuss the "sociology of knowledge" in the next chapter.

Turn now to progressivism, our third philosophy, and ask: How does the advocate of this educational outlook utilize the class idea? In accordance with his operationalist thinking, he refuses to believe that classes are inherently structured by a predetermined world. Rather, he argues that the idea of class is one fruitful way to interpret and analyze our culture, not for the purpose of accepting it, but for the purpose of learning how to examine and modify the class structure where it proves to be unsatisfactory. From this point of view the class structure is not fixed, nor do classes inevitably engage in a dialectic of struggle. Rather, classes are organizations and groupings of people that should be interpreted pluralistically and relatively to the patterns of each culture. Actually, there are various kinds of classes—economic, political, social—and this variety is desirable. A pluralistic culture is potentially a healthy culture where many people do many different things.

For this reason, any kind of dualistic structure of two classes in opposition is unsound, whether the division is determined by economics, races, or status. Dewey's famous definition of democracy as the kind of a cultural arrangement that assures the fullest and freest interaction among all individuals and all groups is enough to reveal why he always opposed the classical economist's defense of the capitalist order. Any culture that centers

power in one class over another class is just as indefensible as
one that assumes that white people are superior to Negro people,
or that men are superior to women, or that one religion is superior to all other religious. For this reason Dewey was not only in
the vanguard of opposition to racially segregated schools, but he
was also opposed to schools for boys alone or girls alone. Schools,
he insisted, should be coeducational on all levels. For similar
reasons he was skeptical of upper-class private schools for the
elite. He recognized, of course, that people have different abilities and different interests, but he favored a social order where
these abilities and interests could share in a continuous process
of mutual enrichment. We might indeed say that progressivism
seems at times to advocate a "transactional approach" to class relationships, just as it does to thinking—an approach in which
classes learn to reduce distances between them by carrying on
transactions to their mutual benefit rather than by engaging in
constant strife.

Another relevant term comes to mind. According to one of
Dewey's most influential disciples, Max Carl Otto, the prime task
of our time so far as class conflict is concerned is to learn how to
practice *creative bargaining* between conflicting groups through
reflective analysis of the motivations that lie behind their behavior. This process is indispensable to democratic relationships in
attacking class conflict. It keeps classes fluid, reduces gaps between them, and does not assume that one class is all right and
another class all wrong.

Yet, just where do progressivists as a whole stand on the class
problem? Their flexibility and openmindedness discourage them
from taking sides too firmly with one class as against another to
the degree that a Marxist would do so—or, for that matter, a
perennialist. True, the student will find that Dewey, in one or
two books (most notably, in *Liberalism and Social Action*), is
much more critical of the exploitative nature of the capitalist
class structure than are many of his disciples—so much so that
he sounds at moments quite Marxian in tone. But this emphasis
is counterbalanced in other writings by so much regard for ex-

perimental processes (he is consistently operational), for plural-
ism, for individual growth, that many of his alleged followers have
preferred "the child-centered school" and similar conceptions—
conceptions almost totally avoiding involvement in explosive issues of class consciousness and class conflict. Certainly, in recent
years, with prosperity and complacency so widespread, one detects relatively meager concern by progressivists with the mili-
tant social features of Dewey's thought. If anything, they have
shied away from this kind of sociocultural interpretation and
toward the safer haven of, say, learning theory.

Now we will discuss reconstructionism. It is only fair to say
that, among the philosophies of education treated in the present
chapter, those associated with this viewpoint are usually the most
willing to admit the influence of Marxism upon their outlook—
the readiest to declare that it might still have something important to tell the world of our day. This does not mean that
reconstructionism is Marxian in its overall beliefs. Indeed, a
Marxist would dislike many of its aspects just as reconstructionism in turn dislikes, for example, the hypostatizations in orthodox
Soviet-oriented treatments of dialectical materialism. What reconstructionists do often affirm is that the Marxian concept of
class enables us to operate upon some of the great conflicts, ex-
ploitations, and inequalities of industrial civilization with a precision of meaning that is otherwise not forthcoming.

It would be impossible to find any such admission in the writings
of the perennialist Hutchins or the essentialist Conant or even in
the great majority of philosophic progressivists such as Boyd H.
Bode. Perhaps it is time that educational theorists did begin to
consider seriously whether such ideas as class, even in a Marxian
context, make any kind of sense.

How, then, may reconstructionists utilize class? First of all,
they may do so by asking whether it helps us operationally (and
here they align completely with progressivists) to obtain more
accurate understanding of why people think as they do or hold
the values they do—whether the high prestige attached to the
successful businessman, for example, is not due to the particular

kind of economic order we have been accustomed to, rather than
to any necessarily more universal justification. (This example
also relates to the cultural issue of relativism versus universalism
discussed in Part II.) Operating with the class concept also has
vast implications for the teacher and learner, as we shall see in
the following chapter; indeed, the teacher may become quite a
different professional person if he allows the class idea to become sufficiently internalized so that he evaluates his own role in
terms of it.

A second way in which the reconstructionist adapts the idea
recalls his strongly axiological emphasis—his primary concern
with the goals of modern education and culture. In one sense, the
great overarching goal of the reconstructionists is, if you wish,
a kind of classless society. Actually, however, Marx and Engels
never spelled out in detail how their ideal order would function.
Hence, they never anticipated the thorny problems that any kind
of reorganized economic, social, and political system must generate. Moreover, their scientific knowledge of human behavior,
individual and group, was far less developed than such knowledge is today. Nevertheless, their vision of a world in which one
class could no longer exploit another class is thus far in accord
with the vision of reconstructionism.

Certainly, the very notion of an international equalitarian culture
is a radical notion—radical in the sense of thoroughgoing and
future-looking. For one to suggest that the supreme goal of our
time must be a continuous series of industrialized democracies
across the globe bound together by a powerful structure of federal authority is to suggest a goal that has never yet been experienced in history—one toward which many young people in our
own country, and no doubt in others, are sure to look with a cyn-
ical eye: "Maybe it's all right in theory; it's impossible in practice."

But reconstructionists reply that only this kind of audacious
democratic radicalism will suffice today. The problem is how to
awaken the school, as a prime agency of enculturation, to the responsibility of challenging youthful cynicism, of stirring learners
to realize the seriousness of our crisis-age, and of moving them

to consider critically but respectfully such disturbing ideas as the classless society and its relevance not only for the United States but for the world as a whole.

One such way of viewing the world situation is in terms of what reconstructionists might term the *forces of expansion* versus the *forces of contraction*. By the latter they mean forces in the world that are organized to promote and preserve the interests of minorities already in power—forces that are sometimes primarily owners of vast tracts of land, oil, or mineral deposits, sometimes primarily religious hierarchies, sometimes political potentates, sometimes a military elite. By the former, they mean those forces that have been struggling to widen their own share of the earth's resources, that are eager and competent to contribute to the rapid industrialization of modern societies across the globe, that are making their voices more and more audible in the deliberations of international bodies such as the United Nations, that are demanding with increasing militancy that they, too, have a right to live, learn, and grow according to the abundant standards long ago attained by the forces of contraction.

The forces of expansion, says the reconstructionist, are now on the march dramatically and sometimes violently in Africa, the Far East, Latin America, and elsewhere. For the first time in the annals of mankind, the African, especially, has found that he, too, can speak so that he is heard far beyond his own tribe and country. Surely, one of the most startling events of the twentieth century was the admission of a whole group of African states to the United Nations in a single ceremony. It was symbolic of the cyclonic rise of downtrodden millions who, for much too long, had been mercilessly exploited by the forces of contraction. No one sensitive to the ubiquity of the class struggles of history could have remained unmoved.

The struggle of the forces of expansion, reconstructionism readily agrees, is fraught with many grave handicaps. Consider the problem of illiteracy. With well over half the people in the world illiterate, how can a world democracy conceivably develop? Here the task, especially of UNESCO, is mountainous.

But, equally, it throws the responsibility squarely upon each of us to decide as teachers where our allegiances lie—on the side of the forces of expansion or on the side of the forces of contraction. The latter forces remain very powerful indeed.

From this viewpoint, one of the burning issues in the second half of our century is whether the remaining noncommunist countries of the world will be able to counteract the powerful appeal of dialectical materialism through a still stronger appeal. The reconstructionist believes that they can do so, but only if education, above all other agencies, enables young people to face the problems of our time honestly and fearlessly, to utilize whatever contributions such ideas as class may have for them, but to do so in the operational mood of experimentation and social consensus rather than by means of a hypostatic doctrine claiming for itself objective reality and indubitable truth.

Conclusion

We have considered two powerful ways of interpreting the class idea philosophically. The hypostatic way produces, according to dialectical materialism, a great ontological system which explains past history, accounts for the present age of conflict, and predicts the future of man. The operational way draws from Marxism those aspects which enable us to utilize class structure, class struggle, class consciousness, as concepts of diagnosis and prognosis in treating ailments of the cultural order. This second alternative requires a great deal of reinterpretation and modification of Marxian theory in its orthodox and still most influential forms.

It is equally possible to approach philosophies of education in terms of the class concept. Perennialism is seen to be an ally of the aristocratic way of life—a normative point of view believing that the primary solution to the problems of our age will not be found until we succeed in developing an elite class after the manner of Plato. The essentialist is an enculturative agent who believes, by and large, in transmitting the allegedly objective laws of the class structure. The progressivist is operational in his use of the class concept, but tends to shy away from any kind of Marxian analysis (although Dewey, more than most, occasionally paralleled it up to a point) because of his pluralistic and operational propensities. The reconstructionist also approaches the class concept operationally, but he reflects more of the Marxian spirit than does typical progressivism when he views the world situation as a vast many-sided conflict between the forces of contraction and the forces of expansion.

In such terms as these, it is even possible to characterize the philosophies of education considered above in broadly political terms. The orientation of the perennialist to class is fundamentally *regressive* because he favors a conception of the class structure that prevailed (with qualifications, of course) in ancient Greece and also in medieval culture. The essentialist is *conservative* because he encourages acceptance of the structure of classes as given by the objective order of the universe and man. The progressivist is *liberal* because he believes in experimentally utilizing classes to increase intelligent transactions and reduce conflicts among all kinds of groups—economic, racial, and religious, among others. Finally, the reconstructionist is *radical*, meaning in this case that modern cultures should move to a clearly envisaged pattern in which, he believes, class exploitation could at last be obliterated—a pattern of democratic relations among all peoples of the world not thus far achieved in the whole of human history.

Recommended Readings for Chapter 7

Bendix, Reinhard, and Lipset, Seymour M., "Karl Marx' Theory of Social Classes," in Bendix and Lipset (eds.), *Class, Status and Power*. Glencoe: Free Press, 1953.

Brameld, Theodore, *A Philosophic Approach to Communism*. Chicago: University of Chicago Press, 1933.

Bode, Boyd H. *Modern Educational Theories*. New York: Macmillan, 1927; *Democracy as a Way of Life*. New York: Macmillan, 1939.

Cassirer, Ernst, *An Essay on Man*. New Haven: Yale University Press, 1944.

Conant, James B., *Education in a Divided World*. Cambridge: Harvard University Press, 1948.

Dewey, John, *Liberalism and Social Action*. New York: Putnam's, 1935.

Eastman, Max, *Marxism: Is It a Science?* New York: Norton, 1940.

Fischer, Louis, *The Life of Lenin*. New York: Harper & Row, 1964.

Hayek, Friedrich A., *The Constitution of Liberty*. Chicago: University of Chicago Press, 1960.

Lenin, Nikolai, *Materialism and Empirio-Criticism*. New York: International Publishers, 1927.

Otto, Max Carl, *Natural Laws and Human Hopes*. New ed. Denver: Swallow, 1957.

8

THE ROLE OF CLASSES
IN EDUCATION

Recapitulation

What significance does the class concept have for us as professional members of the field of education? A great deal, we contend. Some of the implications for teaching, learning, the curriculum, administration, and other facets of school experience have become evident to careful readers of the preceding two chapters. Let us recall their principal theses.

Chapter 6, following the same general model utilized during our study of culture, attempted to epitomize the meaning of class as an explosive idea. In doing so it concentrated, we think properly, on Marx. The first powerful student of that idea in modern social science, he remains even today a fountainhead of fruitful meaning.

This is not to say, we must also reiterate, that Marxian concepts are now accepted without a great deal of criticism and qualification. To be sure, in impressively large areas of the world the Marxian theory of class is much more influential than elsewhere. This is true not only of countries that are governed by Communist or Socialist Parties, but of countries such as France, Italy, England, and Japan, where these parties play a strong minority role.

Social scientists in the United States, while most acknowledge Marx's influence, have given more attention in recent years to what they call the phenomenon of social stratification. A rich literature in the field has developed within a relatively short time, some of it based upon theoretical elaborations of or departures from Marx, others based largely upon empirical investigations.

The meaning of class may be clarified by utilizing again the three chief organizing concepts of culture—order, process, and goals. Although some experts prefer terms such as status to that of class, all of them agree, Marxian or not, that modern culture is organized in terms of vertical layers of social relations. They also agree, by and large, that the vertical order of culture consists of ascending strata, the least economically powerful and usually the least educated strata being at or near the base of the structure, the most powerful strata, economically and politically as well as the most completely educated, being at or near the apex. In the vertical continuum between base and apex are to be found various degrees of power and education associated with the rather amorphous clusterings called the lower- and upper-middle classes.

Process centers here in the dynamics of change within the class structure. We have attempted to show how the two chief process concepts, class consciousness and class struggle, are closely interrelated. At different times and places they range all the way from very subtle to very overt and even violent manifestations.

The concept of cultural goals has been associated in this section with the norm of a classless society. Although not easy to define to everyone's satisfaction—even to Marxists—it does suggest that the target of the class struggle is achievement of a libertarian political-economic-social order where exploitation and hence class divisions based upon exploitation have disappeared.

In the preceding chapter the problem was analyzed on a somewhat deeper level. We centered upon two issues: first, the issue of the hypostatic versus operational approaches to class; second, the issue of how class is incorporated, implicitly or explicitly, into several philosophies of education. The first issue reveals that Marxian theory is characterized to an unusual extent by an admixture of *both* the hypostatic and operational: the former presupposes the objective reality of class structures as well as the inevitability of the process by which they shift from one historical form to another; the latter regards the class concept as an operational instrument for analyzing and controlling crucial types of group relations. Among the four philosophies selected for emphasis, the perennialist and essentialist tend to hypostatize the class structure, its processes, and even its goals; the progressivist and reconstructionist tend to be operational. This difference between the two pairs of theories is by no means absolute, but it does lead to challengingly diverse educational consequences. Some of them now invite more careful examination.

Significance of Class for the School Curriculum

Let us state our most inclusive recommendation first. One of the most needed, yet neglected, areas of knowledge in the typical curriculum, especially on the high school level but to a considerable extent on the college level as well, is that of the meaning of Marxian theory and practice. To be sure, many critics of education have complained at its irresponsibility in not providing typical young men and women with any real understanding of the increasingly powerful movement of communism. Yet, a safe bet is that only one high school senior among perhaps a hundred could accurately define the meaning of, say, dialectical materialism.

What "knowledge" he does possess, moreover, is often distorted and hostile. Thus, when Florida passed a law requiring "study" of communism in every high school, the legislature intended that students should learn about it from a negative and biased viewpoint. This kind of "study" is, we think, worse than nothing. It no more prepares young citizens to evaluate our domestic and foreign policies than does the "study" of the United States by young citizens of the Soviet Union prepare them for intelligent, informed participation in world affairs.

Experimental units in Marxian theory and practice should be attempted in hundreds of curriculums not only throughout the United States but in all democratic countries. For them to succeed, study of original sources will be essential, such as *The Communist Manifesto*, parts of *Das Kapital*, and Lenin's *State and Revolution* (see Recommended Readings for Chapter 5). It means, too, that many teachers will require special in-service training before they can effectively deal with this flamboyant material. Certainly it means that parents and other citizen groups must be kept informed of the nature of such projects, so that they will support it rather than be misled by the kind of "patriotic" pressure groups that are always ready to confuse honest teaching with one-sided, biased indoctrinating. Finally, it means opportunity to meet and hear the views of individuals who are committed to the Marxian philosophy, as well as individuals who are opposed to it.

Actually, teaching and learning about the class structure of America and of other countries, as well as about such processes as class struggle, should be both critical and objective at the same time. Basic weaknesses as well as any basic strengths in Marxian theory should be detected and analyzed. This, of course, also requires the use of expert sources of the kind mentioned in our two preceding chapters—Warner, Mills, Dahrendorf, Veblen, and Hayek, among others. We do not think that selections from such writers are too difficult even for the average high-school student if they are carefully selected and discussed under competent guidance.

The kind of issues to be considered in curriculum projects are exemplified by Leonard Reissman in his *Class in American Society*, a book that demonstrates how class relations are psychological as well as anthropological, sociological, economic, and political. More explicitly, from a Marxian point of view, Oliver Cox in *Caste, Class, and Race* fruitfully examines the intricate connections between race prejudice and class conflict. He also gives extensive attention to the problem of whether or not a caste system exists in America with some similarities to the caste system of India—in our case primarily a Negro caste in the Southern states. His answer is that the concept has limited importance and can often dangerously oversimplify. Warner, among others, has also studied the caste problem, although he is more favorable than Cox to the concept's usefulness.

A word should be said also about the importance of developing class awareness in the elementary school. Without necessarily introducing Marxian concepts, children should begin to recognize their positions in the vertical order of their communities. Some of the effects of membership in, say, the middle class as compared with levels below and above should receive study as indigenous to the study of their culture, as well as other cultures and subcultures.

Learning-Teaching as a Class Problem

Some of the issues that the curriculum should face squarely, but which it now largely avoids, become more dramatic when we turn to a few of many questions that arise when learning and teaching are perceived through the class idea.

Warner, Havighurst, and Loeb in *Who Shall Be Educated?* have demonstrated that the average American teacher is middle class in value orientation. Therefore, the teacher tends both to select subject matters congenial to this orientation and to omit what is uncongenial—for example, the kind of novels required in a high school literature course. Still more significantly, his evaluation of students is likely to be heavily weighted in terms of whether they tend to harmonize with his own notions of what a "nice" or a "good" student should be. One result is frequently not only a more or less unconscious hostility toward students of lower-class backgrounds but a failure to understand their motivations and interests. Nevertheless, we consider this volume an unsatisfactory analysis of the class problem in education. Not only does it continue to blur the distinction between class and status, but to an astonishing degree it encourages acceptance of the prevailing American class structure. Thus, by and large, because it is an invitation to preserve the status quo through education, it is implicitly essentialist.

More will be said below about the significance of the middle-class orientation of teachers. Meanwhile, we turn to the question of the significance of the class concept for learning. The sociologist-anthropologist Allison Davis shows in his *Social-Class Influences Upon Learning* that the so-called intelligence quotient of learners is to a marked degree affected by class background. Contrary to the view still widely maintained in teacher education that the I.Q. is primarily fixed by genetic heredity, the work of Davis, reinforced by that of many others, has increasingly challenged this view and has lent more and more support to the hypothesis that the capacity to learn is radically affected by the cultural environment—especially the class environment— of learners. Thus, when Negro children migrate to the North and their families have greater opportunity to experience social mobility, their intelligence along with their health and general well-being measurably rises—often above the intelligence of whites who remain in their original underprivileged Southern environments.

An accumulation of scientific data is also available proving the close correlation between class level and amount of education. Generally, of course, the higher the class, the more education, regardless of ability. Young people from upper-class homes almost invariably go to college, although many are no more able intellectually than many in the lower classes who are lucky if they finish high school. Also, there seems to be strong evidence that, in America at least, education is itself the most important single criterion for predicting the extent of social mobility; that is, a person of only grade-school education will probably not rise in the vertical order nearly as high as a college graduate. All this is not surprising to most Americans, who have always believed in the power of education to achieve success. Unfortunately, success is often so narrowly conceived in terms of economic affluence that education in turn is geared to the kinds of learning most likely to promote it.

More specifically, we mean by the latter statement that the pressure toward status-seeking affects the selection of subject matters and the formation of habits and values most conducive to upper-class membership. Thus, as young people and their parents recognize how important a college education is to upward mobility, their chief concern, especially in the middle-class suburban communities where more and more of them live, is to assure the kind of curriculum and the kind of academic records that will best guarantee admission to college. Whether these goals are necessarily of most benefit to the emotional and intellectual maturation of learners, and to their later responsibilities as citizens, is of such minor concern to millions of students and parents that it is safe to say the question never occurs to them.

Another connected problem arises from the widespread practice of *homogeneous grouping*. This is the practice of classifying and organizing students according to their differing alleged abilities. Those, therefore, most anxious to climb the class ladder are often anxious likewise to be included in groupings that recognize their ability to learn, say, mathematics or foreign languages more rapidly than those of alleged lower intelligence.

The practice of homogeneous grouping has significant implications for the class problem, in that some culturally minded critics believe it tends to divide schoolchildren into clusterings that intensify attitudes of superiority and inferiority. Such critics of the practice are therefore likely to question its divisive effects—its perhaps unintentional encouragement of a type of subtle segregation which, like all segregation, is inimical to democratic purposes because it sets up barriers to the free flow of human relationships.

This problem, too, is far from easily resolved. Arguments are by no means exclusively on the side of *heterogenous grouping*, which does undoubtedly create learning problems of its own by mixing students of low ability or interest with those of high intelligence. Our main point, however, is that the issue cannot be tackled straightforwardly until it is placed in the context of class structure and of such processes as upward mobility. For example, fruitful research could be conducted to test this kind of hypothesis: homogeneous grouping is advocated more strongly by middle-class and upper-class groups than by lower-class groups primarily because of differing value orientations rather than because the practice is necessarily defensible in terms of more effective learning. (As a matter of fact, research evidence in learning is by no means completely in support of the superiority of homogeneous grouping.)

The learning-teaching dimension of the class idea may finally be considered by way of a fascinating theory called the *sociology of knowledge*. This theory has been influenced directly and indirectly by Marx and Engels. In the briefest possible terms, it attempts to develop the epistemological position that knowledge, at least of the kinds having direct relevance for human relations, is profoundly conditioned by the class position of a given person or group.

To be sure, the contention that what we know is conditioned by who and where we are in the culture is an ancient one. It leads not only to the sociology of knowledge, but to what might be called a "psychiatry of knowledge." The latter could contend that what one claims to know as true is affected by one's emotional patterns, as when a man rationalizes his belief in God to reinforce a personality structure shaped by a strong wish for parental domination.

The sociology of knowledge maintains, however, that personality structures are themselves largely the effect of cultural influences, especially of class influences. Yet, as the theory has been developing over the past thirty years or so, its Marxian origins have been greatly modified by, among others, Max Weber, Veblen and, above all, by Karl Mannheim, a German sociological theorist who completed his life work at the University of London. The full flavor of Mannheim's position can only be appreciated by firsthand study of such books as *Ideology and Utopia*, *Man and Society in an Age of Reconstruction*, and others. We select the key terms "ideology" and "utopia" for particular, although sketchy, interpretation.

For Mannheim, ideology usually refers to the complex of ideas, attitudes, and habits allegedly expressive of the outlook, the beliefs, and the value orientation of a dominant class. In the youth of a given culture, an ideological picture tends more accurately to reflect underlying institutions, policies, and practices than in its later periods of historical development. For what actually happens is that the ideology becomes a kind of encrusted superstructure of symbols (such as newspaper propaganda) overlaying social, economic, political, and other changes that meanwhile continue in the life of the culture beneath the superstructure. Thus an ideology is often reminiscent of *cultural lag*—a concept developed by another famous sociologist, William F. Ogburn.

Schools may also become agents of ideological reinforcement when they portray to the student an image of the underlying culture congenial to the dominant class and power structure. In America, this orientation for much of the past century has, of course, been capitalistic, so that the ideology frequently taught the young is typified by such ideas as individualism, the virtues of competition and free enterprise, and other shibboleths that are likely still to permeate textbooks in our high schools and colleges.

By utopia, Mannheim is not referring to an escape from reality—to castles in the air or dreams of heaven on earth. Rather, the utopian attitude is, in Hegelian terms, a kind of dialectical polarity to the ideological attitude. It may, indeed, function both as critique of and corrective for the obsolescences and distortions that it discovers in the ideological portrait of a given culture.

Sometimes, to be sure, utopian thought points backward to an earlier period of civilization; in such a case it may become a rather nostalgic effort to restore what "once was" because to its advocates this seems more attractive than "what is." More often the utopian orientation tends to be future-looking—that is, it looks ahead toward cultural rejuvenation and tries to specify the nature of the institutions needed for the new order.

Marx (and, to a considerable extent, Mannheim also) was a Utopian of the latter variety. The classless society, previously discussed in terms of cultural goals, is a utopian idea; it is seen both in contrast with and as a substitute for the ideology of a class-structured capitalist society of the sort that has prevailed in most Western cultures for several hundred years.

Education, though it has performed an ideological role in history more often than a utopian one, can and does play the latter role also. Especially in times of tension and accelerating change, utopian-minded educators, often supported by artists and scholars such as, in our own time, the muralist Diego Rivera, the cellist Pablo Casals, and the philosopher of art and society Lewis Mumford, help more and more learners to penetrate the smoke-screen of falsities and cultural lags chronic in typical ideological interpretations. Simultaneously, these educators begin to envisage economic and other cultural arrangements that would alleviate what they consider to be the deficiencies of the traditional order, among them the inequities of social stratification and overconcentration of power in top-level classes.

The potentialities of the sociology of knowledge for both teaching and learning are, we believe, immense. The theory helps teachers to approach the present character of American and world civilization much more critically, and to straighten out some of the warpings that are said to result from ideological control of textbooks as well as of other more popular media of communication and learning. Likewise the utopian attitude, in Mannheim's meaning, may encourage teachers to awaken young people to more audacious and visionary conceptions of the future culture than those to which they have been habituated by the conserving side of the enculturative process.

As the sociologist Robert K. Merton points out, the sociology of knowledge is as yet far from a refined or even consistent theory. Followers of Mannheim need to clarify many remaining difficulties. Nevertheless, as a fresh approach to time-worn epistemological problems and as a tool of practical application to cultural problems, it helps us to face the disquieting argument that knowledge of human beings is by no means a simple matter of gathering facts and drawing generalizations from them. Rather, it is often deeply affected by the perspective from which one looks upon human beings—above all, one's conscious or unconscious class perspective. If the sociologist of knowledge is even partially correct in claiming that a good deal of the teaching and learning that takes place in American and other schools today is crippled by ideological images that more or less conceal or distort underlying changes in the culture, then this alone is sufficient reason to give the theory very careful attention in the professional preparation of every teacher.

The Control of Education: Class Influences

We return to the point above that teachers are overwhelmingly middle class in their value orientation. One of the consequences of this fact is that they do not typically view themselves as working people with the class interests of, let us say, members of a labor organization. On the contrary, studies have shown that most teachers are, if anything, more hostile than friendly toward trade unionism, their own attitudes reflecting the familiar skepticism of such ideological voices as the average newspaper or radio commentator.

One should note, at the same time, that for some fifty years in the United States the American Federation of Teachers has challenged this middle-class orientation. Its own policies have stemmed from the assumption that teachers are white-collar workers and therefore that their best interest will be served if they affiliate with other workers to strengthen their economic position, to protect their academic freedom, and in general to advance the welfare of public education. The AFT is an affiliate of the American Federation of Labor and Congress of Industrial Organizations (AFL-CIO). We should exaggerate to assert that all of its members regard themselves as class-conscious workers. Many remain predominantly middle class in their status values, while recognizing more or less clearly that their economic position and power have much in common with other salary earners, with whom they must organize strongly if they are to advance their professional position.

The AFT reminds us quite correctly that the labor movement has provided strong organizational support to public schools from their beginnings in American history—indeed, that no other organized body of citizens has done so as steadfastly or consistently. The reason is easy to guess: working people cannot usually afford to send their children to private schools, but they do want them to receive educations. Tax-supported public schools are for them the only practical way.

In reply to the familiar argument that it is downgrading and unprofessional for teachers to affiliate with labor, AFT leaders point out that other white-collar workers, such as office and store employees, actors, newspaper writers, and musicians, have their own trade unions—some of them strong and effective. Moreover, the class and status values of such workers are thereby raised rather than lowered: not only, we are told, is their remuneration higher (in Marxian terms, they receive back a larger proportion of the surplus value they produce) so that they can live on a better scale, but they are assured greater security against arbitrary actions by their employers. Also, they are less easily intimidated in their performances and, in general, the services they render attain higher standards of excellence than would be possible if they tried to function simply as individuals.

Thus far, only a small fraction of the teaching profession—perhaps 10 percent—is sufficiently convinced to take the concrete step of affiliating with labor. It is important, therefore, that the issue be examined more thoroughly than is thus far characteristic of schools of education. Particularly, as noted in Chapter 6, it seems essential to inquire whether middle-class *status*, as indicated by Warner's research, is necessarily identical with middle-class *position*. When interpreted in terms of the power structure within American culture and of the economic position that teachers hold in relation to it, the issue is an urgent one.

The problem of educational control is brought into still sharper focus through the class concept when we view critically a cross section of school boards and college trustee corporations. Studies are mutually supporting here also. They show that the vast majority of members are recruited from upper levels of the culture: businessmen, lawyers, physicians, and similar middle-class or upper-class people are far more commonly represented on such boards than are members of the working classes.

The result, of course, is not only that ideological values and customs are reinforced with the sanction of those in highest authority, but that the kind of curriculum encouraged to accelerate upward mobility and admission to college is condoned. By the same token, utopian emphases in the form of critical appraisal of the traditional order or careful treatments of proposals for socioeconomic reorganization are often frowned upon. Equally suspect are aggressive efforts on the part of teachers to strengthen their professional position; it is hardly accidental that the American Federation of Teachers is no more welcome to the majority of school boards than it is to the typical superintendents selected by and responsible to them.

A vivid example of how the problem of educational control may be sharpened by operating with the class concept is the historical pattern of racial segregation especially in the American South. At first glance this pattern may not appear to be a class problem. Yet, discerning scholars have shown that it is so to a large extent—that an underlying if not the primary cause of racial segregation is the Southern agrarian economy that has required for its survival a large pool of cheap exploitable labor. Although the motivation may not always prove to be conscious or deliberate, the fact remains that by keeping Negroes ignorant and weak, by paying menial wages, by providing poor health services and inferior schools, such a pool is assured. From this point of view, the Supreme Court decision of 1954, which declared segregated public education unconstitutional, threatens the entire class structure of the traditional South. When Negro children receive as good an education and as good public services as other children, they are much more likely to grow into adults no longer submissive, no longer tolerant of the exploitative system under which their parents, grandparents, and great grandparents have suffered from slavery onward.

This thesis, too, is more complex than we are able to indicate here. Class factors are by no means the only ones at work. As touched upon previously, some students have tried to show that the idea of caste is even more revealing of the Negro problem in America—that the Negro people are separated from the white people in such a way as to establish a class and power structure *within* their own caste. Thus, Negro teachers may also acquire a middle-class value orientation toward Negro children with all that this implies in their approach to learning and authority. Many other examples are possible.

We conclude our discussion of control by returning to the philosophy of education. Perhaps it is possible to see more clearly than before why, for example, the essentialist may be regarded as an ally of a wider cultural conservatism. Because, with occasional modifications, his hypostatic assumptions encourage habits and attitudes congenial to the inherited order and thus to the class structure within it, we can well understand why essentialist-minded administrators and policy makers welcome this kind of philosophy as a rationale for their own behavior. The efficiently run school is one that emulates an efficiently run business. Rules and procedures follow the traditional line-staff model, with authority centered at the top of the school structure and pointing downward through lines of principals and supervisors to the teaching staff and students. This general model remains the most prevalent one today in both American and European education. It is entirely consistent with the structure of typical profit-making enterprises.

Previously, we observed that the perennialist favors an elite-centered education. It follows that a line-staff model of control is at least as agreeable to him as it is to most essentialists. This fact is easily observable in Roman Catholic parochial school systems where policy is determined by ecclesiastic authority and carried out by teaching personnel, such as nuns, with little or no part in such determination. Among nonecclesiastic perennialists, however, control is regarded not in terms of a theocratic power structure so much as in terms of intellectual superiority. In contrast

also with essentialism, the type of college president or other educational leader demanded by secular perennialists is not measured nearly so much by administrative efficiency as by mature
"rationality"—by the ability to formulate policies based upon
self-evident, universally true principles of truth, goodness, and
reality. Nevertheless, the practical effect is often not only congenial to a class-structured culture, it may also provide a logical
justification for concentration of power in the top echelons of the
educational system, although a power now ostensibly purged of
crass economic or similar "materialistic" motivations.

Progressivists and reconstructionists, as we might anticipate,
favor much greater dispersion of educational authority and direction. Policy boards should be representative of all class levels.
Teachers, students, and parents alike should play important roles
in shaping curricula. Administrators' functions should be more
strictly confined to the responsibilities of operation rather than
of policy making. Reconstructionists, in addition, would favor af-
filiation with the American Federation of Teachers, or of a much
stronger, less equivocal organization dedicated to the democratic
struggle for a world order controlled by the forces of expansion.
While progressivists characteristically appear less certain of themselves on the issue of such an organization, the impulse of both
philosophies of education is to criticize both the ideologically
weighted curriculum of today and the essentialist or perennialist
patterns of authority that help to perpetuate it.

Progressivists and reconstructionists, conceiving of democracy as a society in which power rests unequivocally in the hands
of the majority of people, support the kind of theory of educational control consistent with this position. In short, both points
of view, however much they differ otherwise, regard class as a
concept that helps us to analyze our culture with more penetra-
tion and to interpret education as an innovative process that can
reshape class relations themselves. The vertical order of class
layers, the processes of class conflict, and the goal of a classless
democracy are all subject to precisely the same searching criti-

cisms, modifications, and implementations as any other phenomena of a culture in flux.

Summary

In this chapter we have selected only a few of the rich implications for education that our second potent idea generates. We
have suggested that this idea should receive solid attention in
any curriculum of general education organized around the comprehensive concept of culture. We have urged that the study of
Marxism receive concentrated attention not only in colleges but
in high schools—the kind of attention that treats the theory and
practice of dialectical materialism objectively, respectfully, yet
very critically. The concept of class needs to be extended far beyond the Marxian interpretation, and to be treated in relationship to such significant ideas as status, caste, and race.

As for learning and teaching, the middle-class orientation of
teachers was found to affect not only their approach to subject
matters but their appraisal of the children in their charge. The
influence of class environments upon intelligence and ability has
also been noted, and research evidence has been cited to show
how education both in amount and quality is strongly affected
both by class position and by upward mobility. The class concept
throws fresh light upon the practice of homogeneous grouping
by raising the question of whether it does not help to develop divisive and hence undemocratic attitudes and practices. The last
question raised in regard to learning-teaching was in terms of a
still developing but provocative epistemological theory—the
sociology of knowledge. This theory, please remember, asks
whether truth itself is not often shaped by class forces of ideological or utopian propensity, or both, and hence whether much
of the knowledge taught in our schools is not also surreptitiously
or even openly affected by these forces.

Educational control was reconsidered by means of a disturbing question: Do teachers need to develop a more sophisticated

understanding of their own place in the culture—particularly their social status, as measured by prestige values, and their class status, as measured by their share of economic-political authority? Whether teachers should become conscious of themselves as white-collar workers with class interests comparable to others is a controversial issue to which professional preparation should give critical attention. Equally, the control exercised by governing bodies of schools and colleges may better be understood when their constituent membership is examined in class terms. So, too, may the race problem.

Properly, our major philosophies of education were reintroduced by noting how the essentialist-perennialist partnership, on the one hand, tends to bolster patterns of educational control in accord with traditional upper-class authority. The progressivist-reconstructionist partnership, on the other hand, is not only more critical of the prevailing class pattern but considers ways by which power may be more democratically distributed up and down, as well as across, the entire order of culture.

Recommended Readings for Chapter 8

Cox, Oliver, *Caste, Class, and Race*. New York: Doubleday, 1948.

Davis, Allison, *Social-Class Influences Upon Learning*. Cambridge: Harvard University Press, 1948; *Children of Bondage* (with John Dollard). Washington: American Council on Education, 1940.

Mannheim, Karl, *Ideology and Utopia*. New York: Harcourt, Brace & World, 1936; *Man and Society in an Age of Reconstruction*. New York: Harcourt, Brace & World, 1940.

Merton, Robert K., "Karl Mannheim and the Sociology of Knowledge," in *Social Theory and Social Structure*. Glencoe: Free Press, 1957.

Mumford, Lewis, *The Transformations of Man*. New York: Harper & Row, 1956.

Ogburn, William F. *Social Change*. New York: Huebsch, 1922.

Riesmann, Leonard, *Class in American Society*. Glencoe: Free Press, 1959.

Warner, W. Lloyd, Havighurst, R. J., and Loeb, M. B., *Who Shall Be Educated?* New York: Harper & Row, 1944.

IV

THE EXPLOSIVE IDEA

OF EVOLUTION

9

THE IMPACT OF EVOLUTION

Evolution as a Universal Idea

Evolution is related in many ways to other great ideas, such as culture and class. We need to keep emphasizing this fact of relationship if we are to protect ourselves from the illusion that any of them are born ready-made and self-sufficient. Our study of culture should already have demonstrated how intricate is the network of forces that operate to produce philosophic, scientific, religious, esthetic, and other innovations. In the case of the powerful ideas that we have selected, this network is especially conspicuous, because all of them emerged in their contemporary formulations over a remarkably brief span of time and space. It might even be argued that no one of the three could have assumed the dominant form it has taken without the direct or indirect influence of the other two. But proof of such an argument would require long examination.

It is interesting to recall, nevertheless, how Marx himself welcomed the publication of Charles Darwin's *The Origin of Species* in 1859 as rendering support from the biological sciences for his social theory of class struggle. After all, is not the latter a manifestation of the whole struggle for existence which Darwin emphasized? As a matter of fact, 1859 likewise marked the initial publication of Marx's major theoretical work, *The Critique of Political Economy*. And while the exact year is coincidental, the common mood emanating from both volumes is not. Both were attempting to look at our modern world in the fresh terms of an emerging scientific naturalism. Both were trying to repudiate many of the classical conceptions of animal and man. Both stressed the ubiquitous phenomenon of change. Both were at once "realistic" in facing the "facts of life" and "idealistic" in the ordinary sense of stimulating many readers to envisage the future as potentially more rewarding than the past. Both volumes were indeed explosive—so much so that they continue today to provoke tremendous controversy wherever and whenever one finds them discussed.

The vitality of Darwin's work was dramatized by the centennial celebration in 1959 at the University of Chicago. Hundreds of the world's leading scientists representing not only biology but fields as far apart as astronomy and paleontology spent several days reappraising *The Origin of Species*, reporting on prodigious research that has occurred since its first appearance, and raising issues about which sharp differences remain today. The full report of the celebration is to be found in the three-volume work *Evolution After Darwin*.

Among innumerable startling observations and judgments presented in these volumes, one stands out above all others. Every scientist present, with one qualified exception (we make note of him in Chapter 10) agreed that evolution is a universal phenomenon of nature. Controversies over the concept do not center on its broad scientific meaning. Rather, within the scientific disciplines controversies center upon its implications for further explorations in both theory and research.

Of course, another kind of controversy over evolution continues uninterruptedly among nonscientists, especially between religious viewpoints friendly to science and those that simply refuse to accept the evidence of research because they believe that truth is derived from a totally different source. Here one thinks immediately of the various Christian sects of fundamentalists, such as those who succeeded in passing the notorious law in Tennessee prohibiting the teaching of evolution in the schools of that state. The excellent movie *Inherit the Wind* dramatized the famous trial of Scopes, the young biology teacher who decided to test the law in the courts and was found guilty by a rural jury.

In the respect that millions of people remain ignorant of what is happening in the world of science or who snap their minds shut against whatever scientific knowledge happens to disturb their particular dogmas, even the general idea of evolution is far from commonly accepted today. Among scientists, however, and certainly also among the vast majority of philosophers as well as other scholars in the liberal arts, evolution is a powerful example of an established truth. Yet, it is the kind of truth that opens the minds of men to the pursuit of further truths. In this respect, evolution, too, may be regarded operationally: it is a way of generating continuously expanding meanings about nature and about man's place in nature—especially those meanings relating to processes of change and development.

The two leading figures at the Chicago celebration were Englishmen, both the grandsons of famous exponents of evolution in the nineteenth century: Sir Charles Darwin, himself a distinguished physicist, and Sir Julian Huxley, a biologist, whose grandfather was T. H. Huxley. Sir Julian's definition of evolution is worth repeating. It seems to us to carry much the same authoritative weight as Tylor's famous definition of culture quoted in Chapter 3: "Evolution in the most general terms is a natural process of irreversible change, which generates novelty, variety, and increase of organization: and all reality can be regarded in one aspect as evolution."[*]

Note the provocative terms in this definition. Evolution is not limited to the sphere of living things, but embraces "all reality." Hence, it must extend to the inorganic or prebiological sphere, on the one hand, and to the psychosocial or postbiological sphere, on the other hand.

[*]Julian Huxley, in Sol Tax (ed.), *Evolution After Darwin*, I (Chicago: University of Chicago Press, 1960), 18.

The term "irreversible" suggests that evolutionary changes never lead backward to an earlier state. Nor do they ever merely repeat themselves. On the contrary, they generate "novelty" and "variety." Thus, they occur in time, so that the past constantly modifies the present, and the present constantly modifies the future course of nature.

Yet, evolution is also characterized by "increase of organization." At the same time that it creates an infinite range of new and different forms of nature, it also creates more and more integrated arrangements within and among those forms.

Finally, the term "natural process" deserves special note. The implication here is that evolution can be explained entirely in terms of scientific principles and methods. Nothing extranatural or supernatural is required to account for the processes that bring about those irreversible changes in nature that possess novelty, variety, and increasing organization.

Huxley elaborates his definition at much greater length than we have indicated. He points out, for example, that the preorganic, organic, and postorganic phases of evolution not only succeed each other in time but that each phase has its own characteristic method and each tends to move with successively faster tempo. Educationally, this point has great significance, for at the third or postorganic stage of evolution (the psychosocial stage) man has the capacity to establish and regulate the time factor in evolutionary changes, at least to a degree. Also, he learns how to regulate the preorganic and organic stages; thereby he may affect even their tempo of change. Thus, he is able to improve the stock of plants and animals by scientific breeding. He is even able to bring about deliberate and instantaneous transmutations in atomic structures that might otherwise require millions and millions of years.

The remainder of the chapter provides an outline of the three main phases of evolutionary change. In Chapter 11, we shall return to them as organizing principles for the school curriculum.

Evolution in Preorganic Nature

One of the interesting facts about Darwin's theory of biological evolution is that he was influenced in formulating it by several thinkers who were not themselves biologists. We discuss this observation further on in this section, but here it is pertinent to note that it was a geologist, Charles Lyell, who (if Huxley is correct) encouraged Darwin more than any other scientist and opened up to him the whole idea of slow change in nature—in Lyell's case, of course, change in the physical structure of the earth.

Today the postulate that the entire physical universe evolves is accepted not only by geologists, chemists, and physicists but by astronomers. Speaking at the Chicago conference, Harlow Shapley, a world-famous astronomer, admits that the origin and development of inorganic matter is far from completely understood. He does state that hydrogen is regarded as the primordial element out of which heavier atoms occurred under high temperature and radiation. Helium and oxygen groups were among the early emergents. Certainly, the evolution of matter appears to him as a proper deduction from current theory and investigation.

The breathtaking sweep of imagination that astronomy demands is indicated by the evolution of theories about the scope of the universe itself. Shapley speaks of how puny man becomes in cosmic perspective. The earliest theory in Western civilization, called "anthropocentrism," conceived of man as the center of everything. The second, "geocentrism," regarded the earth as the fulcrum of the solar system with the sun and planets revolving around the earth—the theory of Ptolemy. The third, "heliocentrism," is, of course, the Copernican theory that views the sun as the center of the universe with the earth and planets revolving around it. To some extent, the heliocentric theory still prevails, although actually it, too, is obsolete. A fourth theory, "galactocentrism," which has developed only in the past few decades, is based upon research that reveals our sun to be near the periphery of the Milky Way galaxy, the hub of which is some thirty thousand light-years away from our little solar system.

Galactocentrism also recognizes the evolving nature of galaxies themselves. The universe is constantly expanding. Although the amount of explosion and collision that once occurred has lessened a great deal, there is still a stupendous amount of violent activity. No wonder, if one tries (in vain, we fear) to grasp Shapley's estimate that there are a hundred thousand million billion stars and that over a billion galaxies are already within reach of our telescopes.

Nor is it surprising that astronomers incline to agree that life exists and evolves on countless other planets in countless other solar systems in countless other galaxies. Moreover, while no one thus far knows for sure (we probably very soon shall, thanks to the Space Age), the consensus is widening that the life emerging elsewhere in the Universe is at least partially similar to our own. This deduction is made from evidence that the basic chemical composition of cosmic matter is common everywhere thus far penetrated by spectroscopic analysis. Of course, the precise forms of living things must vary enormously, but "livingness" itself would probably be recognizable because its essential ingredients are already recognizable. Shapley estimates that organic evolution from inorganic evolution has occurred on at least one hundred million other planets.

Here we are brought to the fascinating problem of the origin of life itself. As in the case of the stellar universe, many more questions than not remain unanswered. The Chicago experts who discussed this problem could not, for instance, reach an acceptable definition of exactly what constitutes "life." Yet, they completely agreed that life has evolved from nonliving things and that this has occurred by an entirely natural process. They also agreed that living substances will be made in the science laboratory—or, more precisely, in the highly specialized field of microbiology—but they did not reach unanimity as to when this would occur. One participant held that primitive forms are already being made; another thought that the feat would not succeed until the end of the present century; still another predicted that something less than a thousand years would still be necessary.

All again agreed, however, that a celebrated scientific achievement, sometimes called the Urey-Miller experiments of 1953–54, produced organic compounds under simulated conditions that were quite like those on the earth in its late preorganic stage. Some of these compounds, or parts of them, provide essential ingredients of very simple living substance. But the participants also held that probably the conditions of the earth today are no longer conducive to the natural production of such substances— hence that these can now be produced only artificially by scientific manipulation. Here is a striking example of the way the third stage of evolution may influence the first and second.

Evolution in Organic Nature

We have been discussing the twilight zone between the nonliving and the living—a zone of many subtle steps, only some of which are as yet understood by subcelluar and cellular research. The central impact of evolution results chiefly, of course, from its application to living matter—that is, to the second or organic stage. It was here that Darwin concentrated nearly all of his attention. From it, the idea has widened to embrace both the preorganic stage discussed above and the postorganic stage to be discussed below.

Let us note first that Darwin, no less than Tylor or Marx, was the father of an idea that has since required numerous corrections, modifications, and ramifications. We shall consider one or two of these as we proceed. Our interest now is in the living core of Darwinian theory. This, happily, focuses in a single concept: *natural selection*. Scientists are in wide accord that here is Darwin's supreme contribution. Its meaning, in his own words, is that "any being, if it vary however slightly in any manner profitable to itself, under the complex and sometimes varying conditions of life, will have a better chance of surviving, and thus be *naturally selected*."* In short, qualities that enable a plant or animal to adapt to its environment provide it with greater opportunity to live and reproduce than it otherwise would have. These qualities do not occur suddenly, however; they are typically the result of small-scale processes in large populations and over long periods of time.

The most notable biological discovery since Darwin's own work (his, incidentally, has often been compared in its revolutionary importance with that of Copernicus and Newton) is that the basis of evolution is *heredity*, without which natural selection could not function. The biological qualities most conducive to adaptation, in other words, do not develop through experience or practice or need but are entirely genetic. They occur because the self-reproducing chemical units within living cells, called *genes*, undergo changes the nature of which scientists are still exploring.

According to George G. Simpson, a leading authority on evolution, the "forces" that produce evolutionary change are of three major types. The first is simply the environmental resources (adequate food, say) that enable an organism to grow into a healthy adult capable of reproducing itself. These resources are not themselves sufficient to induce hereditary changes, but they do provide necessary conditions for such changes to occur.

The second is the mechanism of reproduction that not only produces offspring, but offspring always unlike their parents in greater or lesser detail. The changes that thus result are hereditary and are readily observable in the facial features of a human child as compared with those of his father and mother, but they also occur even in the simplest plants and animals. They are due to the vast range of possible combinations between the genes of the parents, some of these combinations continuing more frequently than others in succeeding generations. But, while again impor-

*Charles Darwin, *The Origin of Species*, ed. Morse Peckham (Philadelphia: University of Pennsylvania Press, 1959), p. 74.

tant to the evolutionary process in the respect that those inherited qualities tend to be selected that are favorable to adaptation (a normal physique, for example), no genuinely novel changes in new generations of organisms can result as long as the genetic "sets" remain of the same types inherited from the parents.

Thus, we come to the last and by far the most crucial of the three ways, by comparison with which the first two are, in a sense, subsidiary. This is, of course, the phenomenon of *mutation* by which new kinds of genes emerge. Here the science of genetics is indispensable to the understanding of evolution; although still very young, it has made tremendous strides since Gregor Mendel (the father of genetic science) first tracked down the intricate ways in which mutations operate. We cannot begin to summarize these ways; we can only note a few of the many remarkable facts about them. They occur at random; many more are disadvantageous than advantageous to established habits of life; large mutations are likely to be lethal (a chief reason why geneticists are so fearful of the effects of atomic radiation on all organisms, including the human species); but even single genes or combinations of several genes may, if mutated, modify organic structures.

We are now in a clearer position to understand Darwin's principle of natural selection as it is utilized by present-day genetic evolutionists. The principle must now be understood to mean *differential reproduction*—that is, a process in which all three of the "forces" noted above play a part. If evolution is to occur, first, the environment must permit and encourage the growth and reproduction of healthy offspring; second, the combination of parental genes in the offspring must be conducive to favorable adaptation; and third, the mutations that occur, however slight, must be selected by virtue of their successful adaptation either to an already present environment or to one that is accessible. The evolutionary process thus favors offspring that are most adaptable. But it is "populations" of these offspring that are scientifically important, not individuals. Indeed, the entire process becomes, in a sense, one of statistical averages.

Let us quote Theodosius Dobzhansky, another outstanding

authority, whose book *Mankind Evolving* is a gold mine of knowledge:

> Natural selection is . . . a blind, mechanical, automatic, impersonal process. Its ironclad necessity was clearly expounded by Darwin in an argument that can be reduced to a few sentences. Any organism needs food and other resources in order to live; the resources are always limited. Any species is capable of increasing in a geometric progression; sooner or later the state will be reached when only a part of the progeny will be able to survive. *The statistical probability of survival or elimination, despite accidents, will depend on the degree of adaptedness of individuals and groups to the environment in which they live.* This degree of adaptedness is in part conditioned by the genetic endowment. Therefore, carriers of some *genotypes* [defined as the totality of the genes of an organism] will survive, or will be eliminated, more or less frequently than will the carriers of other genotypes and the succeeding generations will not be descended equally from all the genotypes in the preceding generations, but relatively more from the better adapted ones. Therefore, the incidence of better adapted forms will tend to increase and the incidence of less well adapted ones to decrease.°

Note the terms "adaptedness" and "adapted." Natural selection encourages the production and multiplication of offspring whose hereditary equipment is best able to *adapt* the organism either directly to its immediate environment or to another available environment. When reproduction of offspring thereby gradually leads to differentiation of successive generations, we may say not only that evolution is at work but that it provides direction to the

°Theodosius Dobzhansky, *Mankind Evolving* (New Haven: Yale University Press, 1962), p. 128. Italics added.

process—that is, it gives an advantage to organisms that have inherited genetic changes favorable to adaptation.

Ashley Montagu epitomizes the meaning of differential reproduction in this way: "Those who possess adaptively valuable qualities in their particular environment will be at an advantage in comparison with those who do not possess such qualities, and the former are likely to flourish and the latter not so well."° It follows that the possessors of such qualities tend to leave a more numerous progeny behind them, and so the opportunity for evolution increases as the number of progeny with favorable genetic features increases.

It will be noted that neither of the phrases so often associated with Darwin—"survival of the fittest" and "struggle for existence"—has been quoted. The former phrase retains more respectability today than the latter, which is now largely discarded by evolutionists. Even the former, however, is suspect, for the term "fittest" is ambiguous. Huxley, we observe, uses such terms as "efficient." Simpson speaks of those organisms best integrated with their particular environment. Other experts still allow "fittest" to slip into their discussions. We suggest that part of the ambiguity here is due to the chronic fear of scientists that they are toying with values when they introduce such terms. Here, at any rate, the role of philosophy in appraising the idea of evolution is clearly anticipated (see Chapter 10).

Evolution in Postorganic Nature

Another quotation from Huxley sets the stage for our treatment of the third phase of evolution:

> Though natural selection is an ordering principle, it operates blindly; it pushes life onwards from behind, and brings about improvement automatically, without conscious pur-

---

°Ashley Montagu, *Man: His First Million Years* (Cleveland: World, 1957), p. 52.

pose or any awareness of an aim. Psycho-social selection too acts as an ordering principle. But it pulls man onwards from in front. For it always involves some awareness of an aim, some element of true purpose. Throughout biological evolution the selective mechanism remains essentially unchanged. But in psycho-social evolution the selective mechanism itself evolves as well as its products.*

What move precisely does Huxley mean by the latter kind of "selective mechanism"? In the language of Part II, we prefer to call it the process of enculturation—the capacity of the human species to learn and teach in ways that no other species possesses, its capacity to transmit its experiences from generation to generation in ways that are not genetically inherited but acquired, its capacity also to modify its experiences so that novelty, variety, and increase of organization can occur in a vastly wider range of patterns than anywhere else in our world of living things.

Thus, we are brought back with full force to the idea of culture. Now, however, we are able to view it in fresh perspective—as integral with and an expression of the idea of evolution.

Before we consider this perspective further, a word should be said about another "twilight zone." Earlier we spoke of the still barely explored area between the inorganic and the organic—the area where life begins. Just as scientists agree that the second stage of evolution emerges out of the first, so they equally agree that the third emerges out of the second—hence, that the stage of the culture-building animal, man, is preceded by ancestors intermediate between him and such animal species as the ape. Knowledge of these ancestors is steadily increasing with new discoveries of skull and other bone fragments. For example, paleontologists seem inclined to agree that the *Australepithecus*, while not in the direct evolutionary line that led to man, was closely related to the group that did lead to him.

*Huxley, *op. cit.*, p. 20.

At present, Africa is producing the richest evidence to fill in the gaps, thereby supporting a contention made by Darwin in *The Descent of Man* that our early progenitors probably lived on the African continent. His contention was based on the simple fact that chimpanzees, apes, and other primates are found there in greatest abundance, and that man more closely resembles them than any other living species.

To return to the third stage of evolution, it is promising to observe that biology and anthropology are here beginning to re-inforce each other—still another indication of the increasing co-operation that we have already noted among various sciences. Kroeber, however, notes a crucial difference between biology and anthropology at one point at least—the fact that acquired characteristics can be inherited on the cultural but not the or-ganic level. Culture, he says at the Chicago conference, alters by use and disuse, and all culture is always acquired by the process of learning.

This does not mean that certain aspects of cultural behavior are not explicable in biological terms. Most obvious is the fact that man is a species of animal and, hence, in his biological be-havior is similar to many other species in more ways than he is dissimilar. Much less obvious is another frontier of research: the extent to which genotypes differ within the human species and in turn affect different kinds of cultural behavior. Anthropologists have commonly maintained that human genotypes (those of dif-ferent races, say) make little if any cultural difference as such, since the behavior that results is learned and not inherited. But Simpson, among others, regards this generalization as too sim-ple. Although he would concede a great range of culturally learned similarities that are both actual and potential among all human genotypes, he also asserts that the genotype of Eskimos would impede their adaptation to the culture of tropical pyg-mies. Granting that the example is extreme, it does challenge an assumption widely held, and it calls our attention to the fact that knowledge of human genotypes is very limited.

Still another issue in cultural evolution was anticipated in Part

II. It is whether, as White holds, culture defined in superorganic terms is subject to its own laws of evolutionary development. The issue, we recall, rests on metacultural assumptions and hence must also be clarified with the aid of philosophic criticism. We need not return to it, except to recall that White's premises are those of objective realism and therefore largely nonoperational. His continuous lament that most anthropologists have been anti-evolutionist really means that they have been skeptical of any attempt like his own to hypostatize the laws of cultural change, especially laws that portray the evolution of man as moving in a single "unilinear," more or less predetermined direction. This theory was held by Tylor and by other early anthropologists. Although it has been challenged or modified by many scholars (for example, Julian H. Steward has tried to demonstrate that cultural evolution is "multilinear" rather than "unilinear") it is by no means wholly rejected even today.

The theory that appears to be increasingly congenial, however, is heralded by the quotation from Huxley with which we moved to the psychosocial stage. From this point of view, culture is certainly a product of evolution; moreover, it is itself evolving. But its nature differs from that of the two earlier stages. For example, it is subject to greater human control; it is not so largely the product of random events (though accident and blundering have also played a large part in human history); and, thus, it is even possible to anticipate and plan for future periods in its evolution.

Here the psychological dimension of culture assumes major importance. Kluckhohn is one of a number of anthropologists who contends that most anthropologists have underestimated the role of men in adapting selectively and reshaping their environment. In this position he agrees with another distinguished anthropologist, A. Irving Hallowell, who considers the emergence of the human ego as integral with the whole idea of universal evolution.

The possibilities of directing the course of cultural evolution are fascinating. In this regard, one of the most audacious authorities at the Chicago centennial was Herman J. Muller. Although a geneticist and therefore primarily concerned in his research with the second phase of evolution, he insists that the third phase not only permits but requires interference with the processes that occur through the mechanism of genetic evolution via natural selection. Man, indeed, will become extinct unless he utilizes his "most distinctive characteristic, his foresight" to plan the future of his species. A chief danger lies in the increasing propensity of cultures to preserve and even increase defective genetic structures. A chief hope lies in selective breeding, which is already common in man's improvement of animal species such as cattle. Therefore Muller urges, among other means, artificial insemination for the improvement also of human stocks—a proposal which may shock many of us governed by custom but which, to a geneticist of Muller's stature and imagination, is far more imperative than scientific breeding for better meats or fruits. From now on, he insists, evolution is whatever we make it. Man may disappear into oblivion or he may accelerate his development at a much more rapid pace than trial and error, the usual method thus far, has ever achieved.

In recognizing evolutionary alternatives, Muller is more like Huxley than like superorganic evolutionists such as White. Neither Muller nor Huxley is afraid, for example, of "corrupting" biology or anthropology by psychology simply because they recognize that man possesses intellectual and emotional power to shape his destiny for good or ill. For both scientists, evolution is one of the most powerful instruments ever discovered not only to understand but to direct nature. It does not guarantee the character of the future, however; it only opens the legitimate *possibility* that man can, if he chooses, make his future greater and richer than his past. And he can do so much more rapidly than ever before in the history of the known universe. In Huxley's words: "Instead of reckoning major advance in tens of millions of years," as we must do in speaking of the first two stages of evolution, "we reckon it in centuries."*

---

*Huxley, *op. cit.*, III, 213.

Meanwhile, anthropologists such as Margaret Mead see immediate opportunities for new kinds of detailed research in human behavior as it evolves culturally. One such opportunity lies in still another twilight zone—in the kinds of learning which occur below the level of conscious, verbal communication, and which thus resemble some kinds of nonhuman learning. Here, as in the case of the other two twilight zones discussed above (the beginnings of life and the beginnings of man as a species), evolution reveals "finer gradations within the obvious gross distinctions between cultureless creatures and human beings with culture."*

Conclusion

As has been true of our explorations of the first two ideas, the pages we have devoted to the delineation of evolution could be multiplied indefinitely. A number of important aspects—the role of symbolization at the level of cultural evolution is one example; the strong tendency toward convergence and increasing organization at this level is another—have not been treated. This is why, again and again, we stress the need for further reading in authoritative sources.

In this chapter we have tried to outline the meaning of evolution as a powerful idea by showing how it encompasses not only the organic realm of nature but also the physical and the cultural. The physical realm evolves astronomically, geologically, chemically—indeed, even the expanding galaxies are constantly assuming the characteristics of evolutionary change as defined by Huxley. When we speak of "constantly" we must, of course, reckon in terms of vast distances in both space and time.

The organic realm evolves not only on this planet but in all probability on millions of others. Its common characteristic of

*Margaret Mead, in Anne Roe and George G. Simpson (eds.), *Behavior and Evolution* (New Haven: Yale University Press, 1958), p. 487.

life has itself emerged from the nonliving. The key to the process through which all organisms evolve is differential reproduction, which Darwin clearly recognized but could only partially explain. His own master concept of natural selection combined with genetic mechanisms centering in mutation provides, however, an explanation of organic evolution that is now very widely accepted.

Although anthropologists are not as widely agreed on the mechanisms of the cultural realm as biologists are on those of the organic, they do agree increasingly that evolution is just as applicable to the one as to the other. The most distinctive feature of the third stage centers in the ability of man to enculturate both by way of transmission and of innovation. Here, also, in the view of such geneticists as Muller, arise both immense dangers and promises for the future and thus immense responsibilities for education as well.

Recommended Readings for Chapter 9

Darwin Charles, *The Descent of Man*. New York: Appleton-Century-Crofts, 1896; *The Origin of Species*, ed. Morse Peckham. Philadelphia: University of Pennsylvania Press, 1959.

Dobzhansky, Theodosius, *Mankind Evolving*. New Haven: Yale University Press, 1962.

Hallowell, A. Irving, in Kroeber, Alfred L. (ed.), *Anthropology Today*. Chicago: University of Chicago Press, 1953.

Huxley, Julian, in Tax, Sol (ed.), *Evolution After Darwin*. Vols. I, III. Chicago: University of Chicago Press, 1960.

Kluckhohn, Clyde, *Culture and Behavior*. Glencoe: Free Press, 1962.

Kroeber, Alfred L., in Tax, Sol, *op. cit.*, Vol. II.

Lyell, Charles, *Principles of Geology*. London: Murray, 1834.

Marx, Karl, *The Critique of Political Economy*. Chicago: Kerr, 1904.

Mead, Margaret, *Continuities in Cultural Evolution*. New Haven: Yale University Press, 1964; in Roe, Anne, and Simpson, George G. (eds.), *Behavior and Evolution*. New Haven: Yale University Press, 1958.

Mendel, Gregor, *Mendel's Principles of Heredity*, ed. William Bateson. Cambridge: Cambridge University Press, 1922.

Montagu, Ashley, *Man: His First Million Years*. Cleveland: World, 1957.

Muller, Herman J., in Tax, Sol, *op. cit.*, Vol. II.

Shapley, Harlow, in Tax, Sol, *op. cit.*, Vol. I.

Simpson, George G., "Evolution and Man's Progress," *Daedalus*, Summer, 1961; *This View of Life*. New York: Harcourt, Brace & World, 1964; *The Meaning of Evolution*. New Haven: Yale University Press, 1949.

Steward, Julian H., *Theory of Culture Change*. Urbana: University of Illinois Press, 1955.

10

EVOLUTION AND PHILOSOPHY

The Context of Darwinism

One of Dewey's best-known essays is "The Influence of Darwin on Philosophy." That such influence has been prodigious, few, if any, philosophers would care to deny. A major purpose of this chapter, indeed, is to demonstrate that philosophies of education as diverse as progressivism and essentialism recognize the Darwinian influence as central to their respective outlooks.

Dewey might also have written a second essay entitled "The Influence of Philosophy on Darwin." Particularly if we continue to regard philosophy in wide scope as less an academic specialization than as the way any cultural age seeks to articulate its deepest meanings, we quickly discover that Darwin was very much a man of his age. His assumptions were by no means derived from merely scientific theory or investigation. They were derived at least as fully from the same milieu of European experience that produced, for example, the Marxian and post-Marxian ideas of class.

Let us remember that the decades of the mid-nineteenth century climaxed a period of events long in the making—a period. in which industrial capitalism was fast approaching maturity, a period in which ideas of change and conflict that had been groping for expression were crystallizing, a period of scientific and technological advance that in turn accelerated a growing skepticism toward traditional political, economic, and religious systems.

In this invigorating atmosphere it is not strange that inquiring men should turn toward themselves also, and should ask new and daring questions about themselves. The nature of their role as creators and carriers of culture was one of these questions. A second was their place and function as members of a class-stratified human order. A third was their relations to the rest of nature, including the living world of plants and animals. There were, of course, other disturbing questions.

It is the third question that intrigues us now. Darwin's concern, to be sure, was much wider than with man's origin and development. We have found that his principle of natural selection applies to all living things. Nevertheless, as Jacques Barzun shows in *Darwin, Marx, and Wagner*, the sources of evolutionary theory are at least four: German philosophy, new ways of interpreting history, the physical sciences (recall Lyell's influence), and biology itself—all of them trying in one way or another to picture the world of nature and man in dynamic rather than static terms. The roster of intellectual giants contributing to the picture includes some of the greatest philosophers of modern times, to mention only Hegel, Kant, Schopenhauer, and Mill.

It is not surprising, then, that evolution as a scientific theory should also have occurred to others at about the same time as it did to Darwin. As Kroeber has persuasively argued, the West was so ripe for evolution that it could scarcely have been avoided.

One man, particularly, deserves mention in this regard, although he has been woefully overshadowed by Darwin—Alfred Russel Wallace. This great naturalist independently developed the same basic conception of evolution through natural selection and, indeed, joined with Darwin in announcing it before the Linnaean Society of London. It is also worth noting that Tylor had formed his evolutionary view of culture before he became acquainted with Darwin's work.

Among those directly influencing Darwin, two great figures not hitherto mentioned must now be discussed briefly—Jean Baptiste Lamarck and Thomas R. Malthus. The former not only provided a general conception of evolution as embracing the whole of life, he provided the particular hypothesis that the process occurs through adaptation. Where Lamarck erred, and where Darwin also erred in borrowing from him, was in the contention that evolution can occur through change of habits that, in turn, produce hereditary biological changes. As we have noted, the mistake of both men was understandable, for the science of genetics was still embryonic when they wrote.

Nevertheless, the continuous interpenetration of scientific and philosophic ideas is exemplified here also. While the Lamarckian theory that acquired characteristics can be inherited is rejected by evolutionists virtually everywhere outside the territories under communist control, it is not apparently rejected inside them, During the Stalinist regime, biologists were instructed to proceed according to this theory; after all, was it not in accord with certain of Engels' writings on dialectical materialism? We cannot say how many biologists in these countries ceased to function after the edict, but others—T. D. Lysenko is the most famous—proceeded with botanical experiments for which he claimed proof that Lamarckianism remains basically a valid theory. Lysenko has little if any standing among biologists elsewhere, yet he was promoted during the Khrushchev period to a high-level "scientific" position, thus indicating that he and his associates remain in good standing wherever orthodox Marxism dominates as ideology.

The influence of Malthus is an even more dramatic example of how scientific ideas may be influenced by the cultural climate and by philosophic theories that thrive in it. Darwin had read "for amusement" the *Essay on the Principle of Population* and through it had decided that "the struggle for existence" (Malthus' phrase) was necessary to explain why, through natural selection, some species survived and flourished while some did not. Because population always outruns the food supply, the weaker members of every species must perish.

A plausible case could be made to show that this theory was actually developed to provide a rationale for the industrial revolution that was in full swing during Darwin's lifetime. The severity and ruthlessness of competition, which placed the few in positions of economic superiority and the many in positions of economic inferiority, was justified on the ground that it accorded perfectly with the laws of the struggle for existence. But while it is true that Darwin, through his incorporation of Malthusian doctrine, thereby helped to shape social thought in the decades following 1859 (we shall consider this point again), it is at least equally true, in Montagu's words, that "Darwinian biology was largely influenced by the social and political thought of the first half of the nineteenth century. . . ."*

The context of Darwinism is also enriched by philosophic doctrines that developed during the last half of the century. Marxism, of course, is one of these—in various ways the most powerful of all. But there were other doctrines, several developing at about the same time that Darwin himself wrote, others somewhat later, but all radiating the same virile mood of aggressive change that permeates evolution as a scientific theory.

Frederick Nietzsche, a German professor and contemporary of Darwin, may be chosen as an example. Here is one of the most provocative modern interpreters of man. In a series of passionate books written as much by a poet as by a formal philosopher, Nietzsche repudiates the "weaknesses" that he thinks Christianity encourages with its ethics of brotherhood and gentleness. The human being at his best is an aristocrat who faces danger courageously, who triumphs over life through his "will to power," who is evolving toward far greater capacities than he has ever possessed.

In *Thus Spake Zarathustra* Nietzsche writes:

Man is something that is to be surpassed. What have ye done to surpass man? All beings hitherto have created something beyond themselves; and ye want to be the ebb of

---

*Ashley Montagu, *Darwin: Competition and Cooperation* (New York: Abelard-Schuman 1952), p. 32.

that great tide, and would rather go back to the beast than surpass man? What is the ape to man? A laughing-stock, a thing of shame. And just the same shall man be to the Superman. . . . The Superman is the meaning of the earth. Let your will say: Superman *shall be* the meaning of the earth!*

In this evolutionary conception of man rising to new unimagined levels of power and achievement, Nietzsche is urging man to express his own greatest expectations. But here is an interesting footnote: Nietzsche, although it is said that he was strongly influenced by Darwin, did not approve of some of the implications of the latter's theory. He disliked particularly the Malthusian influence because it seemed to offer an apologia for middle-class Englishmen, of whom Darwin was himself one, and because it seemed to bring man into too close juxtaposition to other animals rather than to glorify man's uniqueness and dignity.

Nietzsche is often badly misinterpreted, as most great philosophers are. Thus, during the reign of Fascism and Nazism in Europe, Hitler and Mussolini both tried to draw upon his works for ideological support—particularly in their doctrines of super-racism. Yet there is little doubt but that Nietzsche would have had nothing but contempt for their corruption of his views, and that he would have been one of the first to recognize how both leaders were caricatures of his own often noble image of the superman.

Another relevant thinker of the last hundred years is the Frenchman Henri Bergson, who was born in that remarkable year 1859 (as was Dewey, incidentally), and who thus grew to intellectual maturity in the heyday of evolutionary thought. Had Bergson been born a hundred years earlier it is inconceivable that he could have produced such works as his famous *Creative Evolution*.

---

*Friedrich Nietzsche, *Thus Spake Zarathustra* (New York: Macmillan, 1924), pp. 6–7.

By this term he means, in essence, that the entire evolutionary process is generated by a primordial life force—the *élan vital*—of which man himself is an expression. Yet we can never really describe this force. We grasp it only by intuition. The intellect is of quite a different nature: it analyzes, delineates, quantifies—and thereby, while rendering important services to fields such as science, it fails to grasp the core of life, indeed its secret.

Bergson's philosophy is a brilliant contribution to the dualistic tradition in philosophy. Man is defined in two parts—his intuitive spirit and his logical intellect, the one vitally energetic with its springs of feeling and creativity, the other static and cold. Creative evolution thus reveals the temporal power of nature and human nature. But in emphasizing nonrational factors so heavily, it seeks to persuade us (as does existentialism later) of how artificial are all ontologies that behold life and reality in purely rational terms.

One other philosopher of evolution, this time an Englishman, will have to suffice by way of sampling. Samuel Alexander, a little younger than either Nietzsche or Bergson, is notable for his monumental *Space, Time, and Deity*. In this work, he tries to unite relativistic physics with evolutionary biology. While space-time is the matrix of all reality, mind is an emergent from it—a view entirely in accord with the three-stage concept of evolution (preorganic, organic, and postorganic) that we have discussed. "Deity" is Alexander's term for a fourth stage of emergence—the unknowable quality of highest value that evolution is able to produce in the space-time continuum.

The purpose of this discussion of "the context of Darwinism" is twofold. First, Darwinism was the effect of strong cultural and philosophic currents flowing across Europe in the second half of the nineteenth century; it could not have developed as it did without those currents. Second, Darwinism was also a cause—that is, it accelerated and crystallized ways of thinking, believing, and acting that were already incipient but were greatly strengthened by its own forceful impact. We continue to develop this generalization in the remainder of this chapter.

Progress and Evolution

Assuming the course of evolution to be universal in nature, can we in any way contend that it is also a *progressive* course—that is, one that moves from a "worse" to a "better" condition than before? In accordance with our policy of selecting only a very few of many philosophic and educational issues that could be raised about each major idea, let us consider this question.

Please remember our fourfold classification of philosophies of education—all of which, we have learned, ramify through philosophies of science, religion, art, politics, and every other dimension of experience. Because the issue of progress is so pervasive, we can be sure that none of the four fails, in some fashion, to consider it.

We begin this time with the most venerable—perennialism. In order to understand its approach to evolution and progress we must also recall two of its important philosophic bases. The first we have termed teleology—the theory that all reality moves toward a final, perfect goal. The second is integral with the first: reality is an eternal unfolding of potentiality toward actuality, of matter toward form.

The father of this theory, Aristotle, seemed to conceive of reality in dynamic terms. Indeed, he has sometimes been regarded as an evolutionist because the forms of nature appear to change. If, however, we mean by evolution what Darwin and his scientific followers meant, then the Aristotelian ontology is not evolutionary. For, according to it, every form that nature manifests on any level from the inanimate to the animate and human is already inherent in reality. Similarly, there is no such thing as explicable novelty because whatever happens in the future lies dormant in the past. For the perennialist, time, indeed, is far less real than timelessness.

As we have seen, it is precisely the fact of novelty and the appearance of temporally new forms that evolution emphasizes. The "actual" changes in form that occur through mutations are not "potential" forms before they occur; they are genuinely new in time. It follows that the future of evolution is not somehow sheltered in the bosom of the past; it, too, is genuinely new. Whether, moreover, one is thinking of the explosions of galactic matter or the biochemical creation of organic mutations, random occurrences are not only common in evolution; they are necessary to its explanation. The Aristotelian, however, can only account for changes in the forms of nature by assuming that they are already latent in lower, less developed forms. It is only our limited knowledge that has prohibited our prior recognition of them.

Present-day perennialists, to be sure, perceive the influence of evolutionary theory and research. Therefore they try to accommodate their own doctrines to it, just as they do other scientific advances in fields such as physics. Here it is enlightening to study the statements of Father J. Franklin Ewing, a Roman Catholic anthropologist; it is he to whom we referred in the preceding chapter as the one partial exception to the consensus of authorities at the Darwin Centennial at Chicago—the consensus that evolution is now accepted as an established scientific truth. Ewing does not discuss the prehuman stages; he does assert that "the scientific validity of the theory of evolution" may be taken for granted. Yet, entirely unlike Huxley, Muller, Kroeber, and the many other scientists present, he goes on to speak of a "spiritualistic evolution" in which man's soul is created by God. Furthermore, although the *Book of Genesis* may properly be reinterpreted in the light of the "literary ways" of the Near East, the "Catholic must be ready to submit to the judgment of the Church" wherever controversy develops between experts in science and experts in theology.*

A far more elaborate and sophisticated attempt to synthesize evolutionary and perennialist thought is that of the Jesuit paleontologist, Teilhard de Chardin. In *The Phenomenon of Man*, he treats evolution as an all-embracing ontology from the physical to the human sphere. In order to do so, he invents provocative

---

*J. Franklin Ewing, in Sol Tax (ed.), *Evolution After Darwin*, III (Chicago: University of Chicago Press, 1960), 19–26.

concepts such as *neogenesis*, to mean the evolutionary emergence of mind; *hominization*, to mean the continuous evolution of man to higher and higher stages; and *Omega Point*, to mean the supreme end of evolution—a point of conscious convergence of the entire cosmic process. The first of these three terms is among many suggestive of Huxley's evolutionary philosophy—so much so, indeed, that he himself has written a glowing introduction to Teilhard's volume. The second reminds us, in some ways, of Nietzsche's "superman," and the third, of Alexander's "Diety."

To return now to the meaning of evolutionary progress for the perennialist, it is surely apparent that this meaning is grounded in his theory of universal order—a theory stemming directly from Aristotle and modified since in only secondary ways. Just as we found culture to be, for perennialism, a progressive unfolding of man's spiritual potentialities, so we now find evolution to be an extension and widening of this same eternal process. It is true that Teilhard (whose major writings, incidentally, were banned by the Church during his lifetime) often writes in ways entirely acceptable to evolutionary scientists. In our judgment, nevertheless, admirers such as Huxley fail to detect sufficiently the perennialist metacultural assumptions upon which Teilhard at least partially builds his brilliant interpretation. No work known to us so successfully incorporates scientific knowledge of universal evolution into a philosophy which, in its most fundamental forms, in nonscientific.

In the more direct terms of educational theory, this philosophy regards evolution comparably to class. That is, it sees reality in general, and human life in particular, as preordained and hierarchical, with rising levels of actualized forms moving toward a final goal of complete spirituality. Within this cosmic structure, education performs the role of drawing forth the "evolutionary" potentialities in man so that his destiny may be realized—eventually and finally the destiny of eternal salvation.

Essentialism, to which we next turn, has been influenced by evolution particularly through what is often referred to as "social Darwinism"—a wonderful example of the ideological utilization of an allegedly scientific theory. As Richard Hofstadter demonstrates in his *Social Darwinism in American Thought*, this doctrine attempts to utilize the struggle for existence and the survival of the fittest to justify the competitive economic system of free enterprise. Here we are reminded, of course, of the influence of Malthusian theory upon Darwin and the later Darwinists.

Of all those who might be selected to illustrate this influence, two names stand out: Herbert Spencer, the English social philosopher, and William Graham Sumner, the American sociologist. Spencer became the intellectual hero of American business leaders, arguing that only the unbridled reign of competition could insure a healthy society. Therefore, all forms of state interference are unnatural, for they violate the laws of evolutionary struggle. It was he, according to Dobzhansky, who coined the phrase "survival of the fittest," which Darwin accepted with some hesitation. Hofstadter quotes the first John D. Rockefeller in Spencerian vein: "The growth of a large business is merely a survival of the fittest. . . . The American Beauty Rose can be produced in the splendor and fragrance which bring cheer to its beholder only by sacrificing the early buds which grow up around it. This is not an evil tendency in business. It is merely the working-out of a law of nature and a law of God."*

Sumner tries to construct a whole sociology on similar premises. "The millionaires are a product of natural selection. . . ," he argues. "There can be no rights against Nature except to get out of her whatever we can, which is only the fact of the struggle for existence stated over again."†

It is unnecessary to argue that all essentialists are as conservative as Spencer and Sumner, or that all social Darwinists were as conservative as they. (The sociologist Lester Ward drew quite different and liberal conclusions from evolutionary theory.) It is equally unnecessary to contend that social Darwinism in its orig-

---

*As quoted in Richard Hofstadter, *Social Darwinism in American Thought* (Philadelphia: University of Pennsylvania Press, 1944), p. 31.

†Hofstadter, *ibid.*, pp. 44, 45.

inal forms is any longer incorporated directly into educational thought. Nevertheless, as we have found earlier, essentialism does maintain that nature and culture are governed by antecedent and irrevocable laws, and that man must learn them in order to accept and obey them. Moreover, these laws often reinforce the dominant power structure and mores of the culture. True, they are not always couched in scientific terms. Yet, as in the quotation from Rockefeller, the "laws of nature" and the "laws of God" often prove to be surprisingly congenial.

Returning to the idea of progress, essentialists by and large believe, then, that a bettering of man's lot is inherent in the course of life precisely because the laws of evolution guarantee it. Education's principal obligation, in turn, is to make sure that such a bettering occurs by the kind of teaching and learning that will not tamper with already established evolutionary processes, but will, on the contrary, condition each generation to function as efficiently as possible in terms of them.

This general outlook is reinforced by ontological realism, the metacultural theory discussed in earlier chapters, which holds that the evolution of culture follows a fairly definite course from "lower" to "higher" forms of human organization—forms that are sometimes referred to successively as *savagery, barbarism,* and *civilization.* An educational philosophy that accepts this kind of superorganicism will, in turn, encourage courses of study that develop beliefs in the inevitability of human progress through these several stages. Spencer strikes the keynote:

> Progress . . . is not an accident, but a necessity. It is a part of nature. . . . As surely as there is any efficacy in educational culture . . . so surely must the human faculties be molded into complete fitness for the social state; so surely must the things we call evil and immorality disappear; so surely must man become perfect.*

---

*As quoted in William H. Kilpatrick, *Philosophy of Education* (New York: Macmillan, 1951), p. 168.

The progressivist theory of evolutionary progress should be fairly clear from previous discussion. Progress does not occur because laws of evolution guarantee it. Rather it occurs only *if and as* human beings choose to make it occur according to their own goals—that is, their own judgments of what constitutes a better human condition than prevailed before—plus their own concerted actions to achieve those goals. Progressivists reject, therefore, not only the perennialist ontology of a universal unfolding of preordained forms, but the essentialist ontology of an objectively structured, law-directed process of evolutionary improvement. In accordance with their operational approach, progressivists regard the idea of evolution in the same way as they regard culture and class—as a useful scientific model to help explain and control the dynamics of a natural world.

This is not to deny that, for educational philosophers of this persuasion, evolution can and should contribute enormously to human progress. Indubitably, it is one of the most fertile ideas ever invented. But its fertility lies in a paradox: by foregoing any absolute assurance of progress, it thereby increases the likelihood that progress can occur. By releasing man, in other words, from the shackles of an already fixed universe, it also releases him to pursue his own course by controlling natural events according to his own ideas of what is most worthwhile.

In Dewey's words, Darwin made us realize as never before that philosophy "foreswears inquiry after absolute origins and absolute finalities in order to explore specific values and the specific conditions that generate them."* Or, as Dewey's great contemporary George Herbert Mead puts it, "The older theory of biology assumed the form already there. . . . This is Aristotelian science. . . . [But] . . . it is possible to conceive of the form of the plant or animal as arising in the existence of the life-process itself. . . . The important thing about the doctrine of evolution is

---

*John Dewey, *The Influence of Darwin on Philosophy* (New York: Holt, Rinehart & Winston, 1910), p. 13.

that the process takes now one form and now another, according to the conditions under which it is going on."*

Educationally, progressivism thus maintains that progress is never certain but always possible. Its possibility depends, in turn, upon one requirement above all others—that enculturation become (as explained in Chapter 4) a process of inquiring and not merely of acquiring. The key to human evolution lies here. Conceived as a way by which men learn to participate in evolution not only on the human level but on those below as well, so does the key to effective education.

In the light of this viewpoint, progressivists such as William H. Kilpatrick do not deny that some kinds of progress have already occurred. Technological progress is most apparent. The control of disease, a greater faith in intelligence, and confidence in man's own power—these also have legitimate claims. For Kilpatrick, the imperative problem of progress is to get the forces of government, morality, art, philosophy, and education to cooperate together and thus to make life better for as many human beings as possible.

Finally, we come to reconstructionism. As should be expected by now, this philosophy, itself a kind of unfinished emergent, follows the progressivist's views of progress, yet seeks to strengthen them. Thus, it also gladly accepts the judgment of Simpson that evolution is by no means always accompanied by progress. Nor is there any discernible purpose in nature which guides progress. Progress as an axiological term has held different meanings for different cultures at different ages, and when philosophers of evolution discover that it is progressing, what they usually mean is that they have projected their own wishes and hopes into the evolutionary process.

This does not preclude the need to decide what progress should mean for our age also. Indeed, the reconstructionist is convinced that such a decision, achieved by as wide a public

*George Herbert Mead, *Movements of Thought in the Nineteenth Century* (Chicago: University of Chicago Press, 1936), pp. 159–66.

consensus as possible, is now imperative. Moreover, education should face the task of sharing directly and aggressively in the determination.

Huxley, we feel, is particularly helpful in strengthening this value orientation. Recall, for example, his "select mechanism" at the stage of psychocultural evolution—"the awareness of an aim, some element of true purpose."

It is precisely this that reconstructionism also stresses, insisting that in our own crisis-culture this purpose centers in the creation of genuine world democracies. Progress, in turn, becomes immediately meaningful because the evolution of culture is once more directional. Commitment to the needed new human order "acts as an ordering principle" and "pulls man onwards from in front."

But it is important to emphasize again that reconstructionists do not develop their theory of progress toward a goal out of thin air. In the language of Chapter 8, they are utopian, yes, but fanciful dreamers, no. What is extraordinary about their radical goal is that it has the support for the first time of a growing body of experimental evidence both for its workability and for its desirability. Muller, for one, comes to mind with his proposals for planned genetic improvement of the human stock. Simpson and Montagu also come to mind—both scientists offering substantial evidence to show, for example, that contrary to Malthus and the social Darwinists, man (like other animals) is far more cooperative than not. In natural selection, says Simpson, "Struggle is sometimes involved, but it usually is not. ... . Advantage in differential reproduction is usually a peaceful process . . . [In] intragroup selection, also, struggle is not necessarily or even usually of the essence. Precisely the opposite, selection in favor of harmonious or cooperative group association, is certainly common."[*]

The significance of such evidence is that it lends substantial strength to the reconstructionist contention that a coopera-

---

[*]George G. Simpson, *The Meaning of Evolution* (New Haven: Yale University Press, 1949), pp. 222–23.

tively organized way of life, from the family to industry to the state and world, is entirely plausible as well as imperative in terms of what we are learning scientifically about the whole of organic nature, including man. Progress in this context is progress toward widening spheres of cooperation. One of education's primary tasks is to translate this conception into exciting classroom and community experience, yet to do so in terms of commitment to the overarching goal of an international cooperative culture.

A Concluding Perspective

The chief purpose of this chapter has been to illustrate how evolution has affected a wide range of philosophic thought, only some of which can easily be classified within our quadruple scheme of educational theories. A closely related purpose has been to demonstrate how evolution as an idea is effect as well as cause—how it is the product of cultural and philosophic influences at the same time that it has helped to shape them.

Throughout these pages, we have also presupposed careful study of the parallel chapters (4 and 7) that deal with the philosophic foundations of culture and class. But we have also tried, in accordance with the aim of cumulative learning, not to repeat any more than necessary of what they sought to accomplish.

Thus, the triadic model of order, process, and goals, while in the background, was not explicitly utilized again. Yet, it would have been possible to do so with the idea of evolution equally as well as with that of our two preceding ideas. Evolution does reveal certain kinds of order, certainly in retrospective study of all three stages—in the development of the solar system, for example, or of the convergence of human institutions. Evolution also reveals very intricate processes—indeed, it exemplifies at least as forcefully as culture how, in reality, order and process are inseparable. As scientifically understood, however, evolution does not reveal preestablished goals. True, as incorporated in certain philosophies—perennialism most, essentialism somewhat—it has been utilized to support teleological or inherently progressive ontologies. But other philosophies such as progressivism do not accept this view. They do, of course, recognize the important role of goals on the cultural level.

Similarly, we have not systematically treated again the hypostatic versus operational ways of explaining the evolutionary concept. Yet, surely it is apparent that both ways permeate philosophies of evolution. Something of the former, it seems to us, lurks in Bergson's and Alexander's thought, something more of the latter perhaps in Nietzsche's. Darwin himself was usually operational, although even he, as Barzun shows, was far from entirely consistent in his philosophy of science. On the whole, the same polarity that prevails in philosophic interpretations of culture and class prevails again here: the perennialist-essentialist continuum tends to hypostatize evolution; the progressivist-reconstructionist tends to be operational. Evolutionary progress is therefore viewed in similarly polaristic fashion.

It would also have been possible to consider evolution more explicitly in terms of the three branches of philosophy. Various ontological theories of evolution have, to be sure, been noted along the way—Teilhard's being an outstanding effort. Likewise, axiological emphases have entered our discussion, especially by way of Huxley. Epistemological dimensions have been noted perhaps least, although touched upon in Bergson's view of two ways of knowing, and again in our reference to evolution through the inquiring process. Here, indeed, is one of the most fruitful of all utilizations of the Darwinian idea—the process of intelligence regarded, not as something separate from evolutionary change, but as integral with it. The human mind, in turn, is understood as the most important mutation by which the human animal, thanks to natural selection, is able to shape the order of evolution, to accelerate its development, and to progress toward human goals that are agreed upon as desirable. Knowledge, in this setting, becomes in turn the chief resource of evolution—and an excellent bridge to our next chapter.

Recommended Readings for Chapter 10

Alexander, Samuel, *Space, Time and Deity*. London: Macmillan, 1920.

Aristotle, *Selections*. New York: Scribner's, 1957.

Barzun, Jacques, *Darwin, Marx and Wagner*. Rev. ed. New York: Doubleday, 1958.

Bergson, Henri, *Creative Evolution*. New York: Holt, Rinehart & Winston, 1913.

Dewey, John, *The Influence of Darwin on Philosophy*. New York: Holt, Rinehart & Winston, 1910.

Engels, Friedrich. *The Origin of the Family*. Chicago: Kerr, 1902.

Ewing, J. Franklin, in Tax, Sol (ed.), *Evolution After Darwin*. Vol. III. Chicago: University of Chicago Press, 1960.

Hofstadter, Richard, *Social Darwinism in American Thought*. Philadelphia: University of Pennsylvania Press, 1944.

Kant, Immanuel, *Selections*. New York: Scribner's 1929.

Kilpatrick, William H., *Philosophy of Education*. New York: Macmillan, 1951.

Lamarck, Jean Baptiste, *Histoire naturelle des animaux san vertèbres*. Paris: Baillière, 1935–45.

Lysenko, T. D., *Heredity and Its Variability*. New York: King's Crown, 1946.

Malthus, Thomas, *Essay on the Principle of Population*. London: Johnson, 1803.

Mead, George Herbert, *Movements of Thought in the Nineteenth Century*. Chicago: University of Chicago Press, 1936.

Mill, John Stuart, *On Liberty*. London: Longmans, Green, 1865.

Montagu, Ashley, *Darwin: Competition and Cooperation*. New York: Abelard-Schuman, 1952.

Nietzsche, Friedrich, *Thus Spake Zarathustra*. New York: Macmillan, 1924.

Schopenhauer, Arthur, *Selections*. New York: Scribner's, 1928.

Simpson, George G., *The Meaning of Evolution*. New Haven: Yale University Press, 1949.

Teilhard de Chardin, P., *The Phenomenon of Man*. New York: Harper & Row, 1959.

Wallace, Alfred Russel, *Contributions to the Theory of Natural Selection in Man*. New York: Macmillan, 1870.

11

EVOLUTION THROUGH EDUCATION

Education, as earlier viewed in enculturative terms, is properly regarded as man's most powerful tool of the evolutionary process. It occurs directly on the postorganic level, but it exerts immense retroactive influence upon the preorganic and organic levels as well.

We propose to select a few of the practical ways in which this influence may be strengthened. Through evolution, the curriculum could be radically improved. Through evolution, our ways of teaching and learning could become far more vigorous and enriching. Through evolution, the control of the school could be developed to harmonize with the principle that man is capable of far greater self-direction and, to recall one of Teilhard's fruitful terms, continuous hominization.

Evolution in the Curriculum

We begin, however, with a discouraging observation. As already noted, evolution, one of the great ideas of all history, is by no means considered a fit subject for the curriculum of some public schools even today. The reason is not that the idea remains scientifically dubious; the reason is entirely cultural. Many communities in our allegedly enlightened United States are dominated by antiscientific and therefore anti-evolutionary ideologies. One result is a sharply curtailed course of study that just as rigidly excludes scholarly attention to the impact of Darwinism upon modern life as it excludes the impact of, say, Marxism.

Simpson, the eminent authority on evolution upon whom we have relied in preceding pages, discusses this scandalous situation in a provocatively entitled chapter, "One Hundred Years Without Darwin Are Enough." It is his contention that "innumerable students still leave high school without ever having heard of evolution, or having heard of it only in such a way as to leave them unimpressed or antagonistic." Because great numbers of people never go further in their education, "this means that an awareness of evolution is lacking or rejected in large segments of the adult population." Such a situation, moreover, is likely to continue so long as incompetent judges are permitted to decide what the curriculum should contain (in this case, usually religious groups, who in turn exert pressure upon governing bodies of the schools) rather than those who are competent to decide (in this case, scientists).[*]

What would scientists themselves be likely to agree are the indispensable principles of evolution to which every educated person should have been exposed? Simpson would, we think, answer: at least the principal ones that thus far have been discussed in this section. Or, paraphrasing his own terms, they would include the following propositions:

1. Man is the comparatively recent product of a natural process that is billions of years old.
2. All living things are related.
3. The principal mechanisms of evolutionary change are now largely understood, and can be formulated as scientific laws.
4. Man's special abilities, such as symbolization, are the product of biological adaptation and hence of natural selection.
5. Mankind is a *kind*, a single species, with its internal resemblances far outweighing its differences.

[*]George Simpson, *This Way of Life* (New York: Harcourt, Brace & World, 1964) p. 36.

To translate each of these generalizations and still others into meaningful terms is, Simpson believes, a formidable task now confronting general education. For one admirable effort toward such translation, we turn next to another top authority previously cited—the great geneticist Muller. It is encouraging indeed that he, no less than Simpson, should take the problem of implementation so seriously as to leave his research laboratory in order to offer educators practical advice.

Muller proposes that evolution become the central integrating theme for the whole of education. Like many others, he is unhappy with the disjointed, piecemeal organization of the typical curriculum. Unlike many others who merely criticize, he suggests that evolution—understood in universal scope—become the unifying category not only for all the physical and biological sciences but even for the humanities. It is a category, moreover, that cuts across subject matters both spatially and temporally, joining together the past, present, and future of man and nature.

Such integration should begin, to be sure, in the elementary school, but Muller pays particular attention to the secondary level. Here he suggests a sequence of three large science courses parallel to the three stages of evolution already considered—the first, in the physical sciences, which would reach from astronomy to chemistry; the second, in the biological sciences, which should pay attention to the origin of life and extend to the most complex forms of physiological and neurological development, culminating in the human brain; the third, in the human sciences, especially those centering in cultural evolution.

At the third stage anthropology is, of course, indispensable, but so too are the humanities—notably, the arts and philosophy. It is interesting that the scientist Muller should pay special tribute to the latter field as indigenous to the evolutionary process. Man as the culture-building animal must, if he is to succeed, have

the wisdom and humanity to choose the true and the good. What is the true and the good then becomes his greatest and deepest problem, but it must be tackled—tackled in the light of all the past and of his new knowledge of the basis of things. In other words, we must become evolution-minded, all of us. . . . One of the main jobs of education should be to open the eyes of our youth to this great ideal, which should serve to orient them and to integrate the mass of otherwise bewildering and seemingly conflicting knowledge that they are expected to assimilate.*

The excitement that such a curriculum could generate in its participants is indicated by a few of the typical themes that Muller would develop:

1. The fascinating connections that appear when the study of the stars is related to the study of geology and chemistry.
2. The distinguishing characteristic of life—its ability to reproduce itself.
3. The rare occurrence of mutations that happen to prove useful to survival.
4. The cooperative nature of animals.
5. The "common urges" of all races and peoples to achieve a happy life.
6. The necessity to regard evolution not as a dogma but as an evidentially grounded concept that yet requires continuous revision and deepening of interpretation.
7. The dangers of human misuse of evolution that can easily result in "mutational erosion—a genetic deterioration"—particularly from nuclear explosions.

Such a visionary design for general education could just as well apply to the undergraduate college as to the high school

*Herman J. Muller, "The Integrational Role of the Evolutionary Approach Throughout Education," *Educational Theory* (October 1960), p. 279.

level. In this and in other respects it recalls the proposal in Chapter 5 for a reconstructed curriculum unified by the idea of culture. The latter proposal differs from Muller's, however, in that all the sciences, even the physical, would be studied in terms of their role in the life of man. Muller's sequence of the physical, biological, and cultural could still be maintained in a culture-centered curriculum. But the vast significance of their evolution would constantly be examined and interpreted in the light of what they mean to the human world of the twentieth century and to the potentialities for good and evil that lie just ahead.

Let us choose one graphic example to highlight our approach—an example with which Muller is himself profoundly concerned. One of the most urgent problems of our age is that of expanding population. Barely a century ago the earth contained one billion human beings. It now contains about three times that many. At the present rate of expansion, it will reach by the year two thousand a total population of over six billions. Note that the number has tripled in the last century, and that it is now expected to double in considerably less than half a century. Each day, one hundred and forty thousand people are added to the total—fifty million per year. The *rate* of increase is thus itself rapidly increasing.

What does this fantastic growth mean and why should the problem be given thorough consideration in the kind of curriculum that we are suggesting? The central answer should not be difficult to find. No responsible public school or college can ignore or soft-pedal any question important to human beings, however controversial. In the case of population, the most controversial question is, of course, family planning and therefore birth control.

The critical need is for frank exhaustive study of how and where such planning can most quickly and effectively occur. The World Population Emergency Campaign, sponsored by dozens of Nobel Prize winners and distinguished leaders, points out that even today two-thirds of the world's people are underfed, and that the most optimistic prospects of enlarged food production cannot begin to keep up with the present rate of population increase.

For reasons such as these, Denmark and Sweden have urged the United Nations to take the lead in examining the scope of the problem and initiating technical assistance especially to countries with abnormally high birthrates. The Campaign's sponsors maintain that a favorable balance of population and resources must soon be achieved. Otherwise the world faces an age of misery, famine, ignorance, and unrest which could generate panic and explode into wars fought over the diminishing means of survival. If this statement sounds extreme, consider one from the scientist, Dobzhansky: "Some of mankind's 'well-wishers' are thrown into a panic by the sharp decline of the death rates. . . . A far greater and more present danger comes from the uncontrolled growth of human populations . . . which threatens to reduce man to starvation and misery."[*]

If, now, we return to one of the three great dimensions of culture—goals—and contend that the curriculum should be governed by the goals required for the world of our time, then clearly the need immediately arises to cope with the shattering import of the statement just quoted. How is it possible to do so, while recognizing with Muller that studies of physical, biological, and cultural evolution are all necessary to a design for modern education?

In answering this question, Huxley, still another of the leading authorities familiar to readers of this section, now becomes helpful. Writing of "Population and Human Fulfillment," he traces the growth of the human race in terms of inventions and discoveries. The evolution of culture has proceeded from the simple food-gathering stage, to organized hunting, to agriculture, to the beginnings of industrial production based chiefly upon manpower and beast-power. All of these stages were accompanied by substantial population growth so that, by the time the industrial

[*]Theodosius Dobzhansky, *Mankind Evolving* (New Haven: Yale University Press, 1962), p. 301.

era had gotten well under way, over half a billion people inhabited the planet.

But by far the most rapid growth has occurred since man learned to control nonhuman power for productive purposes. This period, marked by the technological revolutions in which our own generation is still so deeply involved, has vastly increased the productivity of the earth but, simultaneously, has threatened to overrun the earth with the human beings who multiply with this productivity.

Meanwhile, the medical sciences have advanced also at a prodigious pace, one primary result of which is that life expectancy in some countries has more than doubled in less than one hundred years, while infant mortality has decreased at comparable rates. This double phenomenon, moreover, encompasses wider and wider areas of the world, extending now to almost all of the underdeveloped countries. Thus, as Huxley ironically puts it, humanity is quite suddenly confronted by a race between "birth control" and "death control." The latter, thus far, is way out ahead.

As we look back upon this sketch, it takes but meager effort to see how the entire theme of population expansion is thus bound up with all three major steps of evolution. Not only does the theme afford magnificent opportunity to study, through a single great problem, the main epochs of human history; it affords equal opportunity to study the role of the physical and biological sciences in causing such prodigious expansion. Thus, technology (a name for the partnership of science and industry) has developed a whole new way of life in country after country; consider only the automobile, telephone, radio, airplane, plastics, and electronics. Similarly, without the biological sciences, such phenomenal improvements in health, in reduction of disease, in the quality and quantity of plant and animal food, could not have occurred.

At this juncture, the question of family planning by scientific means becomes not only relevant but unavoidable. As Huxley points out, our knowledge of physiology and biochemistry, working together, has greatly accelerated over merely a few decades. "If we were willing to devote to discovering how to control human reproduction a tenth of the money and scientific brainpower that we did to discovering how to release atomic energy, I would prophesy that we would have the answer within ten years, certainly within a generation."[*]

The reorganized curriculum of general education requires galvanizing, problematic themes to integrate it into powerfully motivating, rewarding experiences in learning. Thus, it appears entirely plausible to develop an experimental design covering, for example, the entire eleventh or twelfth high-school year, the goal of which could be a carefully drawn, dramatic picture of a world population balanced with all necessary resources (food, education, health, and others) in order to assure a humane abundant life for all races and peoples everywhere on earth. The study of history could be organized around Huxley's stages of cultural invention and discovery. Physics, chemistry, biology, and other sciences could be joined in terms of the role of technology and medicine in creating the population crisis. Students would continue, of course, to concentrate in subject-matter areas according to interest and ability. But not a single student could or should be permitted to lose sight of the relations of his specialization to the encompassing theme.

Nor should we forget Muller's appreciation of the place of the humanities. Recall his admonition that the greatest of all human problems is that of choosing the "true and the good"—a problem that demands the inclusion of philosophy (although not necessarily as a formal subject) even on the high school level. This can only mean that axiological aspects of the population question will be omitted from the curriculum only at the expense of intellectual and moral evasion—an omission no less defensible than that of evolution as a whole. The problem of birth control, particularly, is ethical as well as scientific. Thus, while students who

[*]Julian Huxley, *New Bottles for New Wine* (London: Chatto and Windus, 1957), p. 209.

have been taught that the practice is morally wrong are entitled to respect for their beliefs, they are not entitled to ignore the moral problems that unregulated fertility creates. Or, to recall the principle of social consensus (see Chapter 4) as a normative guide to democratic learning, the right of dissent is in itself no justification for exclusion of thorough study of *every* moral issue. The aim, rather, is to examine as fully as possible the evidence concerning all important phases of the population problem, to provide untrammeled communication concerning each phase, and only then to reach as wide and free an agreement among the participating learners as they consider justified in reaching.

Our own view, which we do not expect every reader to share, is that the most defensible consensus that could emerge from this kind of study is one which, on *both* scientific and moral grounds, recognizes the desirability in the years immediately ahead of systematic planning for population growth and for population control. Yet, whether this kind of consensus emerges or not, education has no alternative than to face the questions involved in a mature and unevasive fashion. That some of these questions are very complex is obvious; indeed, here is one of the pressing reasons for dealing with them under genuinely *educational* auspices (whether formal or informal, youth or adult) rather than under the auspices of groups that plead their special case based upon some special interest, such as a particular religious doctrine.

The most pressing reason of all, however, brings us back to evolution and to the central contention of such authorities as Muller, Huxley, Dobzhansky, and Simpson that man alone among all animals on earth has the reflective capacity to shape his own historical course. To be sure, it remains to be seen whether he will utilize this capacity before he commits suicide as a species. Nevertheless, that he does possess it to utilize and improve his lot is of crucial import. In the light of the evidence that we have presented about population trends, the most urgent of all opportunities to do so lies in his largely untested power to control the most primordial of all his drives—the reproductive—on behalf of his long-range welfare. In Huxley's words: "The importance of the population problem for human destiny is now beginning to loom large. . . . If the full development of human individuals and the fulfillment of human possibilities are the overriding aims of our evolution, then any over-population which brings malnutrition and misery . . . is evil."*

Such an outcome of the population explosion is totally unnecessary. But whether man will take advantage of his ability to plan his own course toward the goal of equitable balance before disaster falls is a question which education, understood here as man's most powerful tool of enculturative stabilization and innovation, alone has the potential authority to answer.

Evolution Through Learning and Teaching

A substantial part of the answer depends in turn upon whether learning and teaching can be hitched firmly to the self-directing evolutionary process which lies in man's grasp. Here we are brought back to the concluding paragraph of our preceding chapter, where intelligence was regarded, "not as something separate from evolutionary change, but as integral with it."

Although many authorities in the field of learning would agree with this general statement, they would still not necessarily agree as to the precise function that learning performs as a tool of evolution. Recalling our discussion in Part II, where we sought to delineate certain of the opposing metacultural assumptions of anthropologists, one might, indeed, detect somewhat comparably opposed "metaevolutionary" assumptions underlying the view of those we have cited in the present section.

To clarify the comparison, let us review for a moment. We found that, for some anthropological theorists, learning centers in acquiring, defined essentially as a process of conditioned responses to cultural stimuli. Some other anthropologists are more largely functionalistic—that is, inquiring or creative thinking is

*Huxley, *op. cit.*, p. 306.

for them so characteristic of the human animal that it becomes indigenous to the process of cultural acquiring itself. Philosophies of education tend to reflect the same broad approaches—approaches that, though never as discrete as summary statements might mislead us into supposing, nevertheless invite markedly divergent ways of interpreting the learning-teaching process as a whole.

These divergent ways were anticipated in the last chapter during our discussion of progress. The essentialist in education regards learning and teaching primarily as means of adjustment to evolutionary progress ordained by natural and social laws. The perennialist views the teacher as a "physician of the soul"—one whose task is to draw forth the potentialities of the learner so that he may "evolve" to the highest actuality of which his nature is capable.

The progressivist develops a theory of learning rooted in the trial-and-error behavior of lower animals. But it rejects the extreme behavioristic inference of metacultural and meta-evolutionary theorists (particularly realistic essentialists) who allow little or no place for the creative powers of men to modify by cooperative effort their own evolutionary course. These powers center for progressivism in the function of intelligence—a function at least partially responsible for cultural evolution (although catastrophe, chance, warfare, and other influences must not be minimized) by enabling man to develop more and more scientific, reflective ways of progressing by controlling his environment. The reconstructionist proceeds from this general view of learning to a central concern with the required planetary goals of evolution, in behalf of which education now needs to strengthen and widen the human capacity for intelligent inquiry and concerted action.

Each of these philosophic orientations toward evolution through learning could be spelled out in endless detail. Again, however, we must confine ourselves to only one or two elaborations.

It is helpful, first, to borrow from Solon T. Kimball's interpretation of Darwin's significance for the learning-teaching

process—a significance which Kimball, an educational anthropologist, finds equally as relevant for the present generation as
for that of a century ago. Darwin, according to Kimball, was one
of the great pioneers in the methodology of natural history. This
method, building upon the fact of continuous change, is one with
the scientific way of dealing with problems of nature. It requires
an open mind, precise observation, and concern for the relationships of facts in terms of generalizations. Kimball contends that
Darwin's own ways of learning to interpret nature (a method
which, in our terminology, is intrinsically operational) are applicable to all forms of education from nursery school to the most
technical graduate studies.

For a second and final word on the process of learning and
teaching, we return to Simpson and to some harsh but probably
deserving criticisms of our role as teachers. Too many of us, he
charges, are simply unwilling to believe that evolution is a legitimate idea, even though we may listen politely enough to its scientific interpreters. Others among us accept the idea, but we do
not really intend to incorporate its meaning into our courses of
study because we are too intimidated by or indifferent to the
pressure of community ideologies. Still others of us seek ways
out through compromise: we pay only the briefest possible attention to evolution (and how many textbooks help!) or we stop
short of man, limiting evolution to the lower species, or we treat
the concept as "controversial" which, if one is willing to accept
the consensus of science, it simply is not. None of these compro-
mises, Simpson holds, will any longer do. Education cannot
evade the one legitimate alternative, which is to treat evolution
as a scientific truth comparable to the truth that our solar system
is part of the Milky Way galaxy.

Simpson thus sees the challenge to teaching as severe. Although one might dispute the point, one cannot help but be dis-
turbed by his assertion that there is "no other concept of
comparable importance and scope that has been so slow in permeating education and in obtaining general popular acceptance." To overcome this severe cultural lag,

a great deal of ability and hard work would be required from the teachers. . . . That task will, however, be eased by textbook and curriculum improvements that are currently under way and are among the too few encouraging signs. . . . Still, perhaps an inch or two of progress will result if all those who see the opportunity and the necessity complain loudly enough about the present situation and put themselves productively and courageously to work.*

Educational Control and Evolution

The practical value of Simpson's challenge is that it places squarely upon the profession of education the obligation to determine what is and what is not appropriate for the curriculum, and thus for the student to learn and the teacher to teach. Such an obligation cannot be met as long as public education is controlled by arbitrary administrators, or by prejudiced boards of laymen who forbid thorough and unbiased study of evolution or of any other concept and problem important to an enlightened, democratic citizenry.

This is not the place to discuss in detail how present patterns of educational control can be rebuilt. We only wish to recall preceding comments—for example, in Chapter 8, where the proposal was advanced for a strong, all-inclusive, autonomous organization of teachers with sufficient power to determine the quality and conditions of the service they perform.

But this imperative is not enough. A still more pervasive need is for a comprehensive *theory* of educational control, grounded in the most fundamental knowledge of nature and man available. That typical school and college leaders, such as superintendents and presidents, have thus far lacked such a theory is evident to anyone familiar with current practices in educational administration.

---

*Simpson, *op. cit.*, pp. 40–41.

We do not, of course, contend that thorough understanding of evolution as a concept would in and of itself markedly improve these practices. We do contend that it is indispensable to them—in fact, an excellent norm by which to test the adequacy or inadequacy of professional preparation for leadership roles.

Two of the ways in which this contention may be supported have been discussed under the preceding headings of this chapter. In the first place, the effective leader requires a unifying conception of the curriculum; without it he remains a party to the wholesale proliferation of courses that has been so widely criticized as educational "hash." With it, he possesses a guiding principle (as we have learned that Darwin possessed one) by which subject matter may be compared, integrated, and appraised for their importance to general education. In the second place, the effective leader who grasps the implications of evolution is in a far more defensible position through which to determine what kinds of learning and teaching do or do not contribute to maximum growth and maturity. If he understands, as he certainly should understand, the implications of such conflicting metaevolutionary orientations to the learning process as the essentialist and the progressivist, he will be less likely to support (as he often does now) a hodgepodge of both. Our own expectation, indeed, is that if he recognizes the scientific superiority of a functionalist, progressivist conception of intelligence as the methodology of natural history he will accordingly support a program of learning and teaching grounded in this conception.

He will do more. He will develop an operational principle of control itself—a principle organically related to both of the preceding conceptions. In short, he will develop, defend, and implement a policy of genuinely *democratic* education—the kind of education that recognizes how the postorganic stage of evolution is that stage upon which men not only act the major roles but are the authors of their own drama. By "democratic" we simply mean here a way of life and a cultural order in which the largest possible majority of people "run their own show," establish their own rules, and act together to achieve their own goals.

Building blocks of this theory of human control have been provided by the philosophers and scientists of evolution upon whom we have already relied. With Nietzsche's help, the educational leader could be inspired to conceive of the human species as capable of evolving beyond itself toward much higher levels of development. From Bergson he could learn more deeply to appreciate how man's emergent powers lie not only in rationality but in his *élan vital*, his intuitive creativity. From Alexander and Teilhard he could come to view men more grandly in the vista of a cosmic process in which they express the phenomenon of neogenesis—of mind itself evolving and producing from its own energies ever newer and profounder minds.

From Simpson, Dobzhansky, Muller, Huxley, Kluckhohn, Hallowell, and others of like stature, the leaders of our schools and colleges could acquire the crucial principle expressed in Huxley's term "selective mechanism." By this he means, please remember, the human capacity to pull "onwards from in front" by establishing purposes that enable men to anticipate, to plan, to converge, to shape their own direction, even to improve (through neogenesis) the selective mechanism itself.

That such improvement is not automatic, however, and that it can indeed easily degenerate, is a warning reiterated by these same authorities. The population explosion; the consequences of perpetuating and increasing weaknesses as well as strengths in the human stock; most serious of all, the dangers of genetic damage through nuclear radiation—these are negative factors that no sophisticated educational leader will overlook. Nor will he overlook one of the key contributions of evolutionary realists— namely, that the pre-organic and organic stages *limit* man's capacities; that it is merely tender-minded and romantic to suppose that human freedom to reshape and redirect nature is *un*limited. Hence, we can never ignore the heavy restrictions imposed not only by nature but by cultural habits and mores upon man's innovative drives.

Nevertheless, granting the importance of these counterweights to a balanced approach to educational control, let us not allow them *over*weight. The ultimate consequence of doing so is an essentialist or perennialist theory of control, neither of which in our judgment is in accord with the meta-evolutionary implications that we find in Huxley's principle above.

More specifically, how does this principle point toward a more satisfactory theory? It means, first, that children from the earliest years should begin to acquire the attitude that they are the makers as well as products of nature and culture—shapers of their present and future as well as effects of their past. (This is an attitude that cannot be taught by preachment; it can, however, be slowly incorporated into the character of the normal, growing personality through the way parents and teachers encourage self-reliance, imaginative venturing, continuous sharing.) It means, second, that teachers should become involved at every important stage of curriculum planning, policy making, community cooperation. It means, third, that parents and other citizens should be helped to understand how their schools are enculturative agencies of human evolution. It means, fourth, that education should concern itself centrally rather than just peripherally with the shaping of both far-reaching and convergent cultural purposes appropriate to our age.

In this final mandate we discern the greatest lesson to be learned from our leading authorities on evolution. The future of humanity appears to all of them to be astounding in its fruitful possibilities—a future which it is education's task both to explore and to share fully in realizing. Huxley, for example, writes of the

> need to bring to men's notice the possibilities open to human beings . . . of esthetic and intellectual experience, of more acute perception and awareness, of health, of physical and mental control, of memory, of quick and effective education, of integration. . . . If so, the common man of the future will be ashamed if he does not attain a far higher

level of experience and personality than today's miserable average. . . . *

Simpson reminds us that "we cannot predict for sure whether the future course of human evolution will be upward or downward." But he does plead for a modern ethics that places responsibility on the shoulders of man himself to make sure it will be upward. Such an ethics, however, will not develop fully until we "recognize the supreme importance of knowledge of organic and of social evolution."†

Muller, always audacious in his imaginative projections, is convinced that

> if men do not destroy one another, they will cultivate the deserts, jungles, poles, and oceans, extend their domain successively to ever more distant worlds. . . . Along with the increasing understanding and mastery over physicochemical forces that such expansion implies . . . there will be spectacular progress in means of reshaping and controlling bodily structures and functions . . . and also in means of interrelating people psychologically to achieve higher, more harmonious, and more constructive interactions of their feelings, thoughts, and doings.‡

Dobzhansky, summing up a lifetime of research tempered by the wisdom of philosophy, reminds us that

> Man has not only evolved, he is evolving. This is a source of hope in the abyss of despair . . . Man and man alone knows that the world evolves and that he evolves with it. By chang-

*Huxley, *op. cit.*, p. 123

†George G. Simpson, *The Meaning of Evolution* (New Haven: Yale University Press, 1949), pp. 336–37.

‡Herman J. Muller, in Sol Tax (ed.), *Evolution After Darwin*, II (Chicago: University of Chicago Press, 1960), 457–58.

ing what he knows about the world man changes the world that he knows; and by changing the world in which he lives man changes himself . . . Evolution . . . may conceivably be controlled by man, in accordance with his wisdom and his values.*

The common thread running through these sample quotations is that man, thanks to the mutations that have produced his uniqueness, is correctly regarded not only as the sole culture-building animal but the sole evolution-shaping animal as well. So priceless a capacity is now epitomized in the very term "control." To carry out its fullest possible measure in policies and practices becomes, in the profoundest sense of that term, the first and most solemn of all obligations confronting education.

Toward Synthesis

Our conception of educational control has perhaps sufficiently performed a summarizing function by encompassing within it the principal points developed in our discussion of the curriculum and of learning-teaching. Thereby, we have tried to emphasize that all practical phases of education can be interrelated and bound together by a single great idea—in this case, the idea of evolution.

It remains, however, to underscore the interrelatedness, not only of these practical dimensions, but of the three sequential chapters of this section. No less than in the case of culture or class, we have discovered through the idea of evolution how science, philosophy, and education all fertilize one another. The concept of evolution did not result, for example, merely from the research of Lamarck, Darwin, Wallace, and other biological scientists. It resulted also from the permeating philosophy of the modern Western ethos—so much so that no one interpreter could measure exactly how far the one was primary in its influ-

*Dobzhansky, *op. cit.*, pp. 346–47.

ence over the other. Equally so, education, defined in our terms less as a distinct institution than as the total dynamics of enculturation, played a forceful role: economic, political, esthetic, and other cultural processes were both shaping and being shaped by the processes of informal and formal education.

Even so brief a reference to enculturation should be sufficient to remind us, in turn, that the several aspects of culture need to be interpreted in relation to evolution quite as integrally as the several aspects of evolution need to be interpreted in relation to culture. Nor should we forget here our second explosive idea—class. Please remember, for example, how class is itself a dimension of cultural order; please remember, too, how the values of class at least indirectly affected the work of Darwin (recall the Malthusian influence), and how other interpreters of modern culture (Spencer and Sumner, most famously) utilized evolution to sanction class divisiveness.

Thus, the further we proceed, and the more our web of concepts interwines, the more fully should we come to appreciate the significance, of the contention with which we opened Chapter 7—namely, that the most revealing test of the worth of this book lies in the degree to which the student internalizes its *cumulative* meanings. Each additional link carries along with it all the important preceding links. At times, to be sure, the connections between links are far from obvious; at other times, they are placed in the background of attention; at still other times, we may feel overwhelmed by their complexity. Yet, as each new link is forged, the important question to ask is not whether you or I grasp every connection, for of course we do not. The important question rather is whether, as each of us looks back upon the earlier presentations, they now hold substantially more meaning for us as personalities and as citizens than they did when we began. If they do hold more meaning, we can feel reassured and rewarded for our effort. And so we are better fortified to move ahead toward our responsibilities as members of the educational profession.

Recommended Readings for Chapter 11

Dobzhansky, Theodosius, *Mankind Evolving*. New Haven: Yale University Press, 1962.

Huxley, Julian, *Evolution in Action*. New York: Harper & Row, 1953; *New Bottles for New Wine* (paperback title: *Knowledge, Morality and Destiny*). London: Chatto and Windus, 1957.

Kimball, Solon T., "Darwin and the Future of Education," *Educational Forum*, November 1960.

Muller, Herman J., in Brameld, Theodore, and Elam, Stanley (eds.), *Values in American Education*. Bloomington: Phi Delta Kappa, 1964; in Tax, Sol (ed.), *Evolution After Darwin*. Vol. II. Chicago: University of Chicago Press, 1960; "The Integrational Role of the Evolutionary Approach Throughout Education," *Educational Theory*, October 1960.

Simpson, George G., *This Way of Life*. New York: Harcourt, Brace & World, 1964; *The Meaning of Evolution*. New Haven: Yale University Press, 1949.

V

THE

MULTIDISCIPLINARY

APPROACH TO

EDUCATION

12

AN EMERGING IMAGE OF MAN

"Looking Backward"

Looking backward to the three preceding sections is also to look forward, as in the famous novel by Edward Bellamy, to the creation of a modern image of man. True, the image is by no means a complete one. Much too little, for example, has been said in this book of man's subjective characteristic—of what is sometimes called his "psyche." Unquestionably, the recent development of the science of selfhood, heralded especially by the genius of Freud, is comparable in its impact upon our time to the impact of the three great ideas that we have chosen to interpret. Nevertheless, these ideas, we contend, are crucial to rebuilding a concept of our own species. Moreover, they are at least as indispensable to understanding the nature of the self as understanding of the self is indispensable to them.

Because this is so, the profession of education can no longer afford to neglect them to the degree that it has thus far. Simpson's indictment of the schools for their failure to study evolution effectively could apply almost equally well to the study of culture and class. True, today's teachers can hardly be accused of total ignorance concerning any one of our explosive concepts. The mere fact that all three symbols are commonly used in everyday discourse surely means something. Even so, the neglect of anthropology by typical teacher-preparation curriculums, and almost equally the neglect of all other behavioral sciences except psychology, is evidence enough of gross deficiency. Most teachers of today and tomorrow, even though they may assert that their primary concern is with the growth of the human being, have been afforded relatively meager systematic opportunity to understand him in the way that the scientists and philosophers of modern man are coming to understand him. So long as this is the case, education at any level cannot fulfill the obligations which now press urgently upon it.

What may we find, by taking inventory of our resources, that contributes most abundantly to the emerging image? Let us try to select some, though certainly not all, of the principal features that are both implicit and explicit in the chapters thus far.

What Man Is Not

An ironic commonplace of the social sciences is that people are even slower to modify beliefs about themselves than they are about the rest of nature. One result, which many scholars have pointed out, is that social change in, for example, technological invention usually proceeds at a much more rapid pace than it does in the sphere of customs and morals. Mannheim, whom we studied in connection with class, has developed this thesis by showing how industrial evolution has generated acute need for new social arrangements and commensurate beliefs, which nonetheless lag far behind changes taking place in, say, automatized production.

Thus, it is scarcely surprising that outstanding authorities repeatedly point out how outmoded some of our commonest conceptions of man have now become. A few books listed at the close of this chapter document this assertion from various viewpoints. But all of them converge in agreeing that one of the most serious problems we confront today is that of encrustation of beliefs about ourselves that are no longer scientifically or philosophically defensible.

This is not, obviously, to contend that the convergence is unanimous. Man is much too complex a being ever to expect total agreement about what is or is not his basic nature. Indeed, how dull it would be if unanimity ever were reached: no more questions would need to be asked! Fortunately, we need not worry. However limited, our earlier discussions of disputes among philosophies of education have offered sufficient indication that great ideas are rarely devoid of emotional, intellectual, and social controversy; on the contrary, ideas become great partly because they are so capable of provoking controversy.

As we now review our findings of what man is and what he is not, it is therefore only fair to emphasize that hardly a single statement is completely beyond argument—certainly not in abbreviated form. The reader is reminded, moreover, that this book does not pretend to be impartial; hence, what we shall include, although in every case it has strong authoritative backing, reflects a point of view.

Modern man is anything but static. Hence, we may safely begin our *negative* assessment by declaring that he is by no means a fixed or finished being. This is the case, not only because he himself is part of the evolutionary stream, but because he is the product of cultural patterns and historical conflicts that themselves continually shape and reshape his own development.

Each man, moreover, inherits purely through birth nothing important except his genetic system. He inherits no languages but only the capacity to learn one or more of them. He inherits none of the habits or skills that his progenitors acquired. He inherits no intellectual or emotional qualities that are measurably superior or inferior by virtue of the race to which he belongs. Man in one sense is the cause of culture, for there would be no cultures were it not for him. Yet, in another sense, he is vastly more its effect than he is its cause. Singly, no man, however great his genius, can create a culture.

Considered as a level of nature above the geological and biological (in this sense, superorganic), culture is not an honorific term—that is, it implies no qualities of superior worth. A so-called "cultured" individual who knows Beethoven's symphonies, for example, is no more cultured in the scientific sense than are nonliterate savages who, incidentally, may possess other skills and abilities in some respects superior to his. This is a way of saying that cultures are not limited to so-called "civilizations." Every people has its own culture, and human nature is always, in considerable degree, the product and expression of its particular culture.

At the same time, no culture is ever entirely unique. Each one, even the most isolated, possesses characteristics in common with others—striking numbers of characteristics—and so, therefore, does each of its members. But again, largely because cultures never remain exactly the same from one generation to the next, human nature never remains exactly the same either. Everyone, it has been pointed out, is always like all other men, like some other men, and like no other man.

Nor should we suppose that allegedly primitive cultures are devoid of education. True, some may not possess institutions that are recognized as strictly educational. Yet, none are without practices of learning and of teaching—practices that enable them to transmit characteristics they acquire in the only way that these can be transmitted, but practices also that enable them to modify and invent new ways of behaving. Man is by far the most educable animal on earth.

Similarly, no culture ever studied has been found to lack its own kinds of philosophy, religion, art, and science. Contrary to the notion that "savages" are too stupid to philosophize, too clumsy to create beautiful objects, too "primitive" to appreciate spiritual experience, or too superstitious to solve problems experimentally, we now know that they do all of these things and often wonderfully well. Man is at once philosopher, artist, priest, and scientist.

But it is also true that no members of any culture are identical. This is so not only because, among several reasons, no two persons (not even identical twins) are ever conditioned in exactly the same way by their immediate environments, especially by their families, but also because cultures are nearly always organized so as to divide people into different strata of position and authority. Granting that some relatively "simple" cultures are less stratified than others, it is still a fair generalization that cultures, by and large, are structured into classes. These vary in number, to be sure, and the differences among them in terms of, say, wealth, power, or prestige also vary. The claim of some myth-makers that America is an exception—that our culture is one of equal privilege an opportunity—is false. A corollary of this myth is another—namely, the notion that the public schools of America, being open to all, are not really affected by any class structure and that teachers are rarely if ever influenced in their value judgments of themselves or their students by their own class level in the wider culture.

The negative as well as the positive influence of culture upon education is illustrated further by the extent to which American schools help to perpetuate the social Darwinist ideology of the struggle for existence and the survival of the fittest. Neither view, without such severe qualifications as to deny most of its intent, is now usually considered tenable. And yet, while education contributes its share to preserving the belief that only an aggrandizing profit-motivated economic order can hope to succeed (it alone, after all, is in accord with the "selfishness" inherent in human nature!), education still fails to contribute anything like a responsible share to the facts of the case or, indeed, to understanding evolution as a whole in any legitimate scientific sense.

This legitimate scientific sense has enormous negative as well as positive relevance for the nature of man. It compels us to affirm that evolution can no longer be regarded as a wild conjecture. Nor is evolution necessarily a religious heresy at all. Evolution is a cosmic process rather than limited to the earth alone, and life—the consequence of evolution—is surely not thus limited. Furthermore, evolution demonstrates that man is not a unique species—that, like all other species, he is a product of natural selection. Yet, while man, too, continues to evolve, evolution affirms that he is not automatically progressing toward some higher form. Indeed, evolution is governed by no goal in nature at all—except of course, the goal or goals that he himself creates and then toils to achieve.

Man, in short, finds that no longer is he the center of the universe but only one of its innumerable products. The anthropocentric and egocentric illusions which he long cherished about himself have collapsed along with all preevolutionary doctrines. And yet, as man is thereby forced humbly to reevaluate his own significance, he discovers exciting new resources of insight, knowledge, power, and hope. It is these resources which contribute most to the reshaping of his image.

Reshaping the Image of Man

All of the negative statements encapsulated thus far can be turned around. Restated in *positive* terms, man can be described as dynamic, plastic, growing, evolving. He is as much a natural being as any other consequence of natural processes. He is a single, unified species. His differences, nevertheless, are crucial to him—especially his extraordinary capacity to learn and then to teach what he learns to each new generation. His own nature is molded prodigiously by such teaching and learning. At the same time, he is capable of modifying in cooperation with others the habits and practices of preceding generations. In this way, among others, man endlessly changes as culture also changes.

Man is conditioned not only by the total culture to which he belongs but still more directly by his own subcultures. Family and class, especially, are profoundly influential and contribute much to the fact that people differ from one another even within a seemingly unified culture. True, these influences are often so subtle as to be unrecognized. Class influences, for example, shape attitudes and habits far more than most of us realize. Thus, the findings of science to the effect that the cooperative propensities of animals, including man, are more pervasive than their competitive ones have not thus far prevented education from helping to perpetuate the contrary class-conditioned ideology that often ignores these findings.

Man is not, however, merely an animal conditioned by the processes of acquiring culture. He is capable at the same time of inquiring into those processes—indeed, of inquiring also into the order and goals of culture that are integral with them. This capacity, which leads to philosophy, art, religion, and the scientific method, is epitomized in Cassirer's term for the central differentiating feature of man—his capacity to symbolize. Man, says Cassirer, is the "animal symbolicum." To be sure, man often fails to distinguish between symbols and realities. Thus, to recall an important term from earlier discussion, he tends to hypostatize or objectify his symbols into mythical things. Yet, he also gradually learns to make this distinction—that is, he inquires critically into the habits, events, and practices that he continues to acquire, and he utilizes symbols as marvelously facile aids to such inquiry. Not that he has learned completely to do so even today; too easily and too frequently he reverts to more primitive ways. Even so, it is a reasonable assertion that man's ability to operate with symbols accounts in substantial measure for whatever advances he has made in the course of his long history.

Here, of course, is the great significance of postorganic evolution—the focus of modern man's ontological attention. On this level, and on this level only, he discovers—or at least now begins to discover—that his destiny lies primarily in his hands alone. His inquiring capacity, centering in the discipline of epistemology, enables him not only to analyze but to synthesize; not only to describe, but to prescribe; not only to reexamine what is already present, but to project (and here the symbols of art become peculiarly relevant) imaginative possibilities of what could be present in the future. Thus man, in becoming a goal-seeking being in far more sophisticated ways than is true of other animals, also becomes an axiologist—a searcher for dependable criteria of what is most beautiful and good in life and existence.

But modern man also confronts a major paradox. The very capacity to inquire and to evaluate has enabled him to discover features of his own nature which reveal how limited this capacity often proves to be. He discovers what seem to be demonic forces both in himself and in his culture that try to take possession of his rational powers and to control him in their own behalf.

Freud and Marx, probably more than any other modern students of man's nature, have made us acutely aware of these forces: Freud, in his analysis of the libidinous drives that lie deep in the psyche of every human being; Marx, in his ruthless critique of the conflicts between classes that often unconsciously shape our judgments and actions quite as powerfully as do the volcanic energies within us. Others since Freud and Marx have, of course, qualified and refined their interpretations. Particularly, several existentialists such as Paul Tillich have done so brilliantly with their insistence upon the priority of existence, upon man's ultimate concern with being and nonbeing.

But the fact still remains that we are dealing with a paradox— that is, an apparent contradiction but not a genuine one. The nature of man is *both* fearful and hopeful, *both* rational and irrational, *both* stubbornly resistant to reflective direction and amenable to intelligent judgments of control. The meaning of culture again offers support for this contention. Certainly it is true that man to a large extent is culture-bound. Realization of this truth, however, need not prevent him from discovering how he may, as indeed sooner or later he nearly always does, engage in modifying and thus in innovating the order, processes, and goals of his culture. On the contrary, such a realization is essential to his effectiveness: it requires him to assess the tough obstacles in his path and to develop programs of attack sufficiently powerful to overcome them.

Precisely the same paradox applies to class and evolution. Both concepts enable us to realize more acutely and realistically the enormous strength of the recalcitrant forces that shape human nature. But both, by the same token, help us equally to search for and sometimes to discover the needed strategies by which subjective irrationalities may be controlled, class hostility and class struggle mitigated, and the blind, mechanical, automatic, impersonal process of natural selection directed on the human level on behalf of the highest purposes that man may collectively discover. Man and his world are complementary realities: each shapes and reshapes the nature of the other.

Recommended Readings for Chapter 12

Allport, Gordon, *Becoming*. New Haven: Yale University Press, 1955.

Bellamy, Edward *Looking Backward*. New York: Modern Library, 1942.

Brameld, Theodore, *Education as Power*. New York: Holt, Rinehart & Winston, 1965.

Cassirer, Ernst, *Essay on Man*. New Haven: Yale University Press, 1944.

Dewey, John, *Human Nature and Conduct*. New York: Modern Library, 1930.

Frank, Lawrence K., *Nature and Human Nature*. New Brunswick: Rutgers University Press, 1951.

Frankel, Charles, *The Case for Modern Man*. New York: Harper & Row, 1956.

Freud, Sigmund, *Civilization and Its Discontents*. London: Hogarth, 1953.

Fromm, Erich, *Man for Himself*. New York: Holt, Rinehart & Winston, 1947.

Jaspers, Karl, *The Future of Mankind*. Chicago: University of Chicago Press, 1961.

Kluckhohn, Clyde, and Murray, Henry A. (eds.), *Personality in Nature, Society, and Culture*. Rev. ed. New York: Knopf, 1953.

Malinowski, Bronislaw, *Freedom and Civilization*. New York: Roy, 1944.

Maslow, Abraham (ed.), *New Knowledge of Human Values*. New York: Harper & Row, 1959.

Mumford, Lewis, *The Transformations of Man*. New York: Harper & Row, 1956.

Tillich, Paul, *The Courage to Be*. New Haven: Yale University Press, 1952.

Whyte, L. L., *The Next Development in Man*. New York: Holt, Rinehart & Winston, 1948.

13

MANDATE TO EDUCATION

What Is Education's Purpose?

Although the preoccupation of contemporary education with mastery of imposed subject matters, achievement testing, and college entrance requirements may cause us to overlook the fact, these were never the primary ends for which education has evolved as an institution.

In the bright light of philosophy, the arts, and now, above all, the social sciences, education has been found to be governed by much more pervasive ends. These are revealed in the comprehensive meaning of the term "enculturation"—the universal process by which people living in cultures arrange (1) to transmit what is most important in their way of life from one generation to the next, and (2) to engage in amending and renewing these ways whenever they perceive that change is necessary to the common good.

What we are saying, simply, is that the central purpose of education is constantly one: the universal welfare of man living in culture. And because all others are secondary and instrumental to this purpose, any system of education that so obscures it as to place subjects, drills, grades, testings, and promotions in the foreground of attention has forgotten its basic role. Rather, it becomes a system that suffers acutely from the confusions and reversals of ends and means.

If, however, the life of man in all its complexity is the foremost purpose of education, then, clearly, the profession of education needs to understand above all what *this* "subject matter" encompasses. As we have discovered in these pages, such understanding is anything but easy to obtain. Most imperatively, it requires a defensible image of man himself—an image derived from the most reliable knowledge obtainable of science, art, and philosophy, yet an image that is admittedly never complete, hence an image that is fraught with controversial aspects, but certainly an image that, in basic respects, is radically different from the one that we have inherited from periods of history preceding our own.

This is not at all to say that *knowledge* of man is itself ever enough. The first business of education is to translate this knowledge into meaningful teaching and learning and thereby to channel it into practice and experience. Nor is this to deny that other kinds of knowledge are essential besides those which directly involve man: of course the physical sciences, for example, must occupy an important place in the curriculum. What we do stress again, however, is that standard subject matters and skills are for the most part instrumental to the central purpose—that is, they are resources through which man may more effectively develop himself in a community of men. When they become ends in themselves, as they too often do, their instrumental value becomes so exclusive that education loses sight of the purpose for which they were provided in the first place. Sometimes, as a consequence, they remain in the curriculum far beyond the time when they might have served such a purpose. Today, particularly, the questions persist: To what extent does education organize its programs consistently and directly in terms of the problems and needs of human beings? To what extent does education neglect these problems and needs because of obsolescent habits and cultural lags?

Preceding chapters have tried to illustrate how education would be altered if such ideas as culture, class, and evolution were allowed to permeate our schools and colleges. The reader is urged at this juncture to review these illustrations in order to see how all of them, directly or indirectly, reflect and express the conception of modern man that begins to crystallize from them.

Here, we need only be reminded that the curriculum becomes most importantly a curriculum in *human order*, that learning and teaching become *human processes* by which students engage in both attacking weaknesses in that order and in correcting them by ameliorative measures, and finally, that the control of education becomes first of all a way to achieve the great *human goals* of our age through participation by the largest possible membership of its major enculturative agency.

Education as Transmission and Innovation

We have frequently said that education as this agency performs two reciprocal roles—one, that of transmitting cultural order and, two that of modifying and even altering this order. It has also been agreed that, traditionally at least, the former of these roles has often appeared to be the more conspicuous.

Let us emphasize once more that the transmissive role of education is entirely legitimate—indeed, an essential one. No culture could survive unless means for its perpetuation through the process of acquiring were sufficiently provided. But let us also emphasize once more that the conclusion often drawn from this assertion by proponents of a conservative philosophy of education is an invalid one—namely, that because education has always performed a transmissive function, this must inevitably be its primary if not its sole function. Cultural evolution shows the facts to be otherwise. Even the most rigid cultures are compelled sooner or later to modify themselves or to be modified by others. Education, defined in its cultural sense, inevitably participates in these activities.

Periods of history greatly differ, to be sure, in the range of their resistance to or encouragement of change. So, therefore, does education. In some ways we are passing through a period today of exceptional resistance. While few deny that extraordinary changes now occur virtually everywhere on earth, it is as though some of those in powerful positions to influence ideologies would have education try to conceal such changes from the younger generations. It is as though the schools, or at least many schools, were trying to persuade students that beneath the surface of technological, social, and moral innovation everything is secure.

Our own view, on the contrary, has been that to the extent this kind of persuasion occurs in education, it is wrong and should be challenged. Just because ours is a time of innovation that is drastic in its effects upon every aspect of life, upon every corner of the globe, education has exactly the opposite responsibility from that supported by conservative apologists. This is the responsibility of enlisting education in the accelerating processes that are now prevailing—enlisting it not only by helping every learner to become much more aware of their revolutionary implications, but by sharing in the direction of these processes.

The word to underscore is *sharing*. Of course, education cannot singlehandedly bring about sweeping economic, political, moral, religious, or any other kind of change. It can, however, *in concert with* the institutions most involved in change, perform a very powerful function—far more powerful than it has ever performed thus far.

Will the educational profession grasp this opportunity? We cannot really say. Innumerable difficulties confront its doing so, some of which have been pointed out. In the context of earlier chapters, the most serious are the obsolescences and gaps in the image of the human being himself—he who is, after all, the prime object of education. Other difficulties (the habit of conformity among some teachers is but one) have hardly been touched upon.

Yet, it is equally apparent that many members of the profession, both those in preparation and those seasoned with experience, are eager and ready to participate in the adventure that education for cultural renewal portends. To these fellow members this book is primarily addressed. It reminds them, moreover, that there are many precedents. After all, people throughout history have been venturing forth: trying, erring, trying again, seeking better ways of life, crossing bridges that link with their immediate experiences.

The Model of Three Bridges

We conclude with this familiar metaphor. Our book began by picturing the applied discipline of the philosophy of education as a bridge that connects two other bridges—on one side, the arts and sciences; on the other, educational practice. Incessant traffic moves both ways across the three-bridge span, to and from the myriad ways of life that constitute the history and the struggles of humanity.

Teachers and students, too, need to join in the crossing. The risks that they take are well worth the cost. The record of man is awesome and wonderful—filled though it is with defeats as well as victories, miseries as well as joys, cruelties as well as kindnesses. The image of modern man is awesome and wonderful, too. Yet, with the knowledge and experience that we now possess, it could become far more so than it has ever been. Man the *culture-building animal*, man the *class-conscious animal*, man the *evolution-directing animal*, man the *symbolizing animal*, now grasps the potentials of self-knowledge with which to remake his world. Education can and should share in this remaking.